Forces of Change
Artists of the Arab World

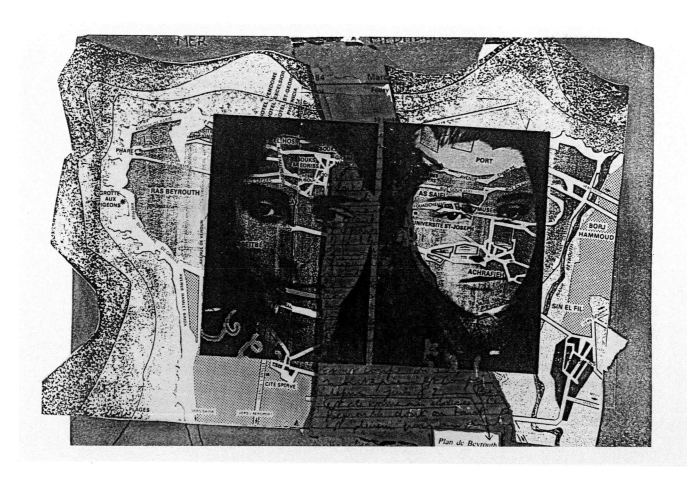

Forces of Change
Artists of the Arab World

Salwa Mikdadi Nashashibi

Additional contributors:
Laura Nader
Etel Adnan
Shehira Doss Davezac
Todd B. Porterfield
Wijdan Ali

The International Council for Women in the Arts
Lafayette, California

The National Museum of Women in the Arts
Washington, D.C.

1994

This catalogue accompanies the traveling exhibition *Forces of Change: Artists of the Arab World*, organized by The International Council for Women in the Arts.

Exhibition Schedule:
The National Museum of Women in the Arts
Washington, D.C.
February 7, 1993–May 15, 1994

Dudley House, Lehman Hall, Harvard University
Cambridge, Massachusetts
May 27–June 30, 1994

Wolfson Gallery and Central Gallery
Miami-Dade College, Miami, Florida
January 13–February 25, 1995

Gwinett Fine Arts Center, Atlanta, Georgia
March 14–May 7, 1995

Editors: Brett Topping and Nancy Lutz
Designer: Susan Rabin Design, Baltimore, Md.
Typesetter: BG Composition, Baltimore, Md.
Printer: Schneidereith & Sons, Baltimore, Md.

Cover: Leila Kawash, *Diaspora*, 1992 (detail), mixed media collage on canvas, 36 × 30 in. Collection of the artist. Photo by Mark Gulezian.

Frontispiece: Ginane Makki Bacho, *The Image of the Word, The Image of the Picture*, 1985, artist's book, hand-colored prints, 11½ × 15½ in. Collection of the artist. Photo by Mark Gulezian.

The photograph on page 65, *6596 SCÈNES ET TYPES.—La Cruche fêlée.—LE* was taken from Malek Alloula, *The Colonial Harem*, trans. Myrna Godzich and Wlad Godzich (Minneapolis: University of Minnesota Press), Theory and History of Literature, vol. 21. Copyright © 1986 by the University of Minnesota. All images in *The Colonial Harem* are from the collection of the author.

Library of Congress Cataloging-in-Publication Data
Forces of change: artists of the Arab world / Salwa
    Mikdadi Nashashibi…[et al.].
        p. cm.
    Exhibition catalog.
    ISBN 0-940979-26-8
    1. Art, Arab–Exhibitions. 2. Art, Modern–20th
century–Arab countries–Exhibitions. 3. Women
artists–Arab countries–Exhibitions. 4. Feminism
and art–Arab countries–Exhibitions. I. Nashashibi,
Salwa Mikdadi, 1948-   . II. International Council for
Women in the Arts. III. National Museum of Women
in the Arts (U.S.).
N7265.3.F67 1994
704'.042'09174927–dc20   93-47447
                                                CIP

ISBN 0-940979-26-8 (softcover)
ISBN 0-940979-27-6 (hardcover)

© 1994 The International Council for Women in the Arts, Lafayette, Calif., and The National Museum of Women in the Arts, Washington, D.C.

Note concerning the Arab terms used in the essays: Words or names that have a familiar English form are used in that form. Other names for which there are two or three possible spellings have been transliterated in accordance with the system established by the *Dictionary of Modern Written Arabic*.

Contents

Acknowledgments

The exhibition, educational programs and catalogue have been made possible by the following major contributors and others whose support is very much appreciated:

INDIVIDUALS: His Majesty Sultan Qabus of Oman, His Excellency Prince Talal Bin Abdel Aziz al-Saud, Mr. and Mrs. Mohsen al-Qattan, an anonymous contributor, Mr. Haseeb Sabagh, Mr. Izzat Saeb Nashashibi, Mrs. Lorraine Grace, Dr. and Mrs. Frank Agrama, Mrs. Sawsan Lababidi, Mrs. Latifa Kosta, Mr. Mohammad Imran and Her Royal Highness Princess Taghrid Mohammad.

FOUNDATIONS AND CORPORATIONS: Arab Bank PLC, Mr. and Mrs. Maximilian Hoffman Foundation, Post-Apollo Press, Arab American Cultural Foundation, National Association of Arab Americans, The Middle East Institute's U.S. Outreach Fund, The Middle East Policy Council, Saudi ARAMCO and the Arab Women's Society of Georgia.

On behalf of the International Council for Women in the Arts (ICWA), The National Museum of Women in the Arts (NMWA) and all those who helped develop this project, our special thanks to Her Majesty Queen Noor al-Hussein for her unwavering support for the exhibition and for rallying the support of others. We would also like to acknowledge all the Arab embassies who have actively supported this exhibition, and ICWA's committees, representatives and contacts in the Arab World, Europe and the United States. For their unstinting assistance abroad we would like to thank the following. ALGERIA: Malika Bouabdallah, Director of the National Museum of Fine Arts in Algiers, and her staff members Nouredine Farroukhi and Dalila Orfali. EGYPT: His Excellency Dr. Farouk Husni, Dr. Layla Takla, Dr. Ahmad Nawar, Ms. Bahira Mukhtar, Dr. Mamdooh Biltagi and all members of the ICWA committee in Egypt for facilitating the gathering and custom's release of the artwork and excellent media coverage on the exhibition during the Project Director's stay in Egypt; Ghada Dajani at the Modern English School, Hasna Mikdashi and many others who helped in the research and assembly of the artwork; the Adham Center for Communication at the American University in Cairo; Emmad Allam and his crew for photography services; and Egypt Air for providing air travel for one person from Cairo to Washington. ENGLAND: Mai Ghousoub, Maysoon al-Hashemi, Lubna el-Miqdadi and Rose Issa for assisting in research and catalogue photography. FRANCE: Dr. Ibrahim Alaoui for his valuable assistance; Layla al-Wahidi and Marie-Claude Behna for their assistance in research; Diala Hamzeh for facilitating our stay in France and acting as translator. JORDAN: The Royal Jordanian Airlines for shipping thirty-five pieces of artwork assembled in Jordan from neighboring Arab countries. We are particularly grateful to The Jordan National Gallery of Fine Arts for donating the costs of assembling, storing, cataloguing and crating thirty-five pieces of artwork; Aramex for donating courier service between Jordan and the United States; Jordan-French Insurance Company for insuring the shipment from Jordan; Fuad Mimi for taping the interviews with the artists; and the Jordan National Television for providing the camera and crew. LEBANON: Middle East Airlines for shipping Mrs. Saloua Raouda Choucair's artwork; Motaz Dajani for his assistance in videotaping interviews and contacting artists. MOROCCO: Pauline Demazieres and Sylvie Bel-Hassan for their professional advice on the project since its inception, and Mohammad el-Miqdadi for coordinating our stay in Morocco.

We thank the following institutions and individuals for agreeing to lend paintings to the exhibition: L'Institut du Monde Arabe, the Jordan National Gallery of Fine Arts, Errol Karim Aksoy Foundation, the Estate of Her Royal Highness Princess Fahrelnissa Zeid, Mrs. Gulperie I. Sabry Abdallah, Mrs. Raya Jallad, Mr. and Mrs. Esmat Halawa, His Royal Highness Prince Talal Bin Mohammad, Mr. Nazir al-Sati, Mr. Jack Shea, Dr. and Mrs. Frank Agrama, Mrs. Jan M. Lilac, Mr. and Mrs. Khaled Shoman and Mrs. Hala Kittani.

This show is complex and multifaceted. We are grateful to all those who assisted in all its aspects, from fund-raising to gathering research materials and locating venues for the traveling exhibition. We are indebted to the work of Exhibition Director Salwa Mikdadi Nashashibi, whose vision and dedication made this exhibition a reality. We especially acknowledge NMWA's Founder, Wilhelmina Holladay, for her pioneering outreach to the international art community. Our thanks also to NMWA Director Rebecca Phillips Abbott for her help in planning the exhibition. Others at NMWA who deserve special mention include Susan Fisher Sterling for her curatorial guidance in all facets of this complex project and her profound knowledge of the arts, which provided invaluable help. For her positive encouragement to the exhibition since its inception we thank Krystyna Wasserman. Many thanks also to all staff members who worked patiently with us, accommodating endless inquiries and adjustments.

Our thanks go to the exhibition advisory committee who participated in the selection of the artwork exhibited: Dr. Wijdan Ali, Prof. Shehira Davezac, Dr. Roy Sieber and Dr. Susan Fisher Sterling. We also greatly appreciate the contributions of the catalogue essayists: Laura Nader from the University of California, Berkeley; author and poet Etel Adnan; Shehira Davezac of Indiana University, Bloomington; Todd B. Porterfield from Princeton University; and Wijdan Ali, founder and director of the Jordan National Gallery of Fine Arts.

We are especially grateful to those who have worked on a regular basis with Exhibition Director Salwa Nashashibi: fellow board members Laura Nader, Etel Adnan and Lola Grace, as well as other staff members of ICWA who have worked on the project at various stages.

We are also indebted to Leila Gorchev, Karen Abu-Hamdeh, Angelle Khachadoorian, Linda Pitcher, Giti Sepahi, Maigan Van Wagenen, Heather Tunis, Osama Abusitta and Souhad Ameen Rafey. We thank Prof. Davezac for making a special trip to California to advise and assist. We are grateful to Samia Halaby for her help in editing the biographies. We appreciate Nabila Mango's help in the transliteration of Arabic names. We thank Nadia Hijab for her help in organizing the symposium, and Zuheir al-Faqih for directing and editing the video interviews. We would also like to recognize two volunteers who accompanied the Exhibition Director on a recent trip, helping to videotape and transcribe interviews with artists: Mona Nashashibi and Guilian Riley. In addition, we extend our thanks to all those who have in one way or another been involved in the project whom we cannot name personally. Our thanks to all the artists who have shared with us not only their art but also their valuable experiences which led to its creation.

The International Council
for Women in the Arts

The National Museum
of Women in the Arts

Finally, this exhibition and the catalogue would not have been possible without the unfailing support and appreciation of my husband, Izzat S. Nashashibi, and our children, Omar, Nadia and Ramzi Nashashibi. For the last five years the children have grown up with this exhibition and shared their vacations with it, visiting museums and artists. I hope they will one day appreciate and value these experiences as a worthy investment of their time, making them more aware of Arab culture. I also would like to recognize the historian Darweesh el-Miqdadi, my father, who invested his students and children with a lasting appreciation of their history and culture. A special note of appreciation is due to a woman who was a pioneer in the field of education in Kuwait, Rabiha Dajani, my mother. She facilitated a great number of the initial contacts to locate many of the artists presented in this show. To them, and to all other friends and family members who helped so much with this exhibition through their assistance and their patience, thank you.

Salwa Mikdadi Nashashibi
Exhibition Director

Preface

The concept of "forces of change" is rooted in my abiding interest in Arab women's artistic expression. At an early age I was impressed by the textile and embroidery traditions of the Arab region. In the late 1960s, while I attended college in Beirut, my fascination with creative expression led me to become involved with the local arts community. Over the years I have maintained contact with the artists I met during that time, and this network provided the starting point for the research that followed.

In recent decades women in the Arab world have played a major role in creating and fostering art. The Lebanese arts scene provides one example of the types of activities in which women have been engaged. Beirut offered a wealth of arts events in the 1960s with the opening of several new galleries, including Gallery One, founded by the poet Yusif al-Khal and his artist wife, Helen Khal. Another center that drew many young artists and presented excellent cultural programs was Dar el-Fan, founded in 1967 by the late Janine Rubeiz. During the Lebanese civil war the center continued its activity in Mrs. Rubeiz's apartment, where she exhibited many fine artists.

In earlier decades women established several centers which promoted the traditional arts and crafts of Lebanon and provided the public with opportunities to appreciate and explore the country's indigenous arts. Lodi Edde founded the first such center in the 1930s. Others followed later—such as Inash el-Mukhayem, established by Huguette Caland and Shermine Heneine, and The Artisans, started by May Khoury. These efforts not only created jobs for Lebanese craftspeople but also provided support for Palestinian women living in refugee camps.

In other Arab countries women also have initiated and supported projects in the arts. For example, Najah al-Attar is presently the Minister of Culture in Syria, and Sheikha Hussa al-Salem al-Sabah established the Dar-al-Athar al-Islamiyyah Museum in Kuwait with an impressive collection of Islamic art objects.

In Jordan, Princess Wijdan Ali founded the Jordan National Gallery of Fine Arts in 1980 with the largest permanent collection of contemporary Islamic art in the world. Ali also organized a comprehensive exhibition of contemporary Islamic art at the Barbican Centre, London, in 1989. Recently Suha Shoman established the Darat-al-Funun, a haven for art and artists in Jordan. The center houses a permanent art gallery, a library and a studio. This studio provides the opportunity to explore new fields in the arts that require specialized technical equipment and creates an environment in which artists can interact and exchange ideas.

The late Inji Efflatoun of Egypt organized the exhibition *Egyptian Women Painters Over Half a Century* for the Year of the Woman in 1975. In Alexandria, several women artists were among the first to frequent independent workshops.

In Tunisia, Safiyyah Farḥāt established the Radeis Art Center in her family home. There she encourages the creation of woven tapestries with contemporary designs.

Malika Bouabdallah in Algeria has been the Director of the National Museum of Fine Arts for several years. The first contemporary art gallery in Morocco was founded by Pauline Demazieres.

Leila al-Attar, Director of the Iraqi Center for the Arts in Baghdad for over two decades, organized the largest exhibition of work by Arab artists ever presented. Her tragic death during the recent bombing attack on Baghdad was a major loss to the Arab art world. These women and the work in this exhibition testify to the pivotal role of Arab women in the arts. There are few fields in which women have participated and contributed as much.

Through courses in the Art Department of the American University of Beirut I was introduced to women such as Saloua Raouda Choucair and Jumana el-Husseini who were establishing new trends in the arts. Artists were in the forefront of political and social consciousness. After the 1967 War, Mona Saudi, a Jordanian artist living in Beirut, published a collection of artwork by Palestinian children, *In Time of War: Children Testify* (1970). This book drew attention to children's ability to express their reactions to life in the refugee camps and to war.

I also had an opportunity to collaborate with Wadad Kawar in the mid-1960s in developing a collection of traditional Palestinian costumes. Over the last three decades Kawar has continued to gather and catalog Palestinian textiles and jewelry. Her efforts insured the preservation of this rich cultural heritage of the Palestinian people.

In the early 1970s I emigrated to the United States, where I often received requests to organize exhibitions of women's traditional arts—weaving, embroidery and costume shows. I found a lack of books which illustrated the diverse creativity of Arab women of yesterday and today. By contrast, readily available was an array of books and articles on Arab women which perpetuated the stereotypes held in the West, including publications by 19th- and 20th-century European travelers who described the intimate lives of women in harems. This one-dimensional interest in a region with a population of over 200 million challenged me to provide other resources and activities focusing on the contributions of Arab women to their contemporary cultures.

In 1985, while planning an exhibition of artists from the region, I realized that no single comprehensive source of information existed on Arab women artists. Past research on the subject was limited to a few specific countries: Helen Khal's *The Woman Artist in Lebanon* (1976) or the more recent book by Nazli

Madkour, *Women and Art in Egypt* (1993). This prompted my investigation. Several trips to the region followed, during which I met with artists, gallery owners, directors of contemporary art centers and museums, professors of art and art collectors. These trips seemed always too short, given the territory and the material to cover. The contacts I established were of great help to me in continuing to develop a comprehensive database on the artists.

In 1989 The National Museum of Women in the Arts (NMWA) contacted me for assistance in updating their library files on Arab women artists. NMWA was the first museum in the United States to include data on Arab women artists in its archives. From that initial interest this exhibition, *Forces of Change: Artists of the Arab World*, developed.

In 1990 Laura Nader, Etel Adnan, Lola Grace and others joined me in the founding of The International Council for Women in the Arts (ICWA). ICWA maintains a resource database with information on women artists who are seldom represented in the United States. This resource is available to museums and art institutions in the United States and abroad.

After four years of research and collecting slides, tapes, texts and videotapes, it was possible to mount an ambitious display. The resulting exhibition gives wide coverage to the diversity of the cultures in the Arab world. Presented are works from the last fifty years, with an emphasis on the more experimental and nonacademic trends of the past fifteen years.

The exhibition and its catalogue provide an introduction to contemporary Arab art for the American public and convey the ideas and concerns of Arab artists. An advisory committee that included both Arab and American reviewers selected the artwork. The principal themes which have come to the fore in assembling the works are: FORCES OF CHANGE—the problems of daily life, civil war and armed conflict, human rights, occupation and the environment; PRESENT REFLECTIONS—the influence of contemporary art movements in the Arab world and the more conceptual work created in the last fifty years; RHYTHMS OF THE PAST—artists' exploration of earlier artistic expressions and their creation of personal statements using local materials and symbols of the past; and IMAGE AND THE WORD—

contemporary forms and interpretations of Arabic calligraphy and the use of the written word as a mode of visual expression.

To collect the required information for an exhibition from a region of twenty-one countries, I personally met with and interviewed most of the participating artists, as well as others whose work was of interest. The artists included in the show come from Algeria, Bahrain, Egypt, Iraq, Jordan, Kuwait, Lebanon, Morocco, Oman, the Palestinian West Bank and Gaza, Saudi Arabia, Syria, Sudan, Tunisia and the United Arab Emirates. Others are of Arab origin now living in the United States and Europe. Unfortunately, due to space limitations, we were are unable to include all deserving artists, or artists working in photography and textiles.

Although I was familiar with the historical and cultural influences which are the foundations of contemporary art in the Arab world, my direct contact with the artists deepened my understanding of the uniqueness of their creative expression. Interviewing the artists in their homes brought out the realities of their struggles and achievements. Their stories were punctuated by their reactions to wars, pollution, emigration, marriage, child rearing, divorce, financial worries and problems specific to the artistic profession.

The Western world is starting to open up to Arab contemporary art. In the last decade the British Museum has built a collection of works by Arab artists. The French public now regularly attends shows of Arab artists organized by L'Institut du Monde Arabe in Paris, an organization sponsored by France and countries of the Arab world. *Forces of Change* communicates Arab women's growing sense of power. Theirs is neither a neglected spirit nor an oppressed one. Their contributions to art are bringing them recognition and financial rewards, in their own countries and abroad.

Art invites the viewer to go beyond stereotypes. In the popular culture of the United States, the media rarely looks beyond the conflicts and disasters of the world to convey the significance of people's daily lives and aspirations. Thus, upon hearing about *Forces of Change*, an Egyptian cabinet minister declared, "At last! Someone is coming from America to report something positive about our country. We welcome so many visitors with open arms, and when they go back home all they write of is children playing in garbage or people living in graveyards in the City of the Dead!"

Prevalent American scholarship on Arab art usually focuses on the pharaonic and the medieval periods. Knowledge of the contemporary artistic production of the region has remained scant, however. We think that this exhibition is the first major step toward making contemporary Arab art equally as well known, as well as stimulating further interest and scholarship. The art in the exhibition is intended to elicit admiration, outrage and amusement. Most of all, though, it is intended to communicate.

Salwa Mikdadi Nashashibi
Exhibition Director

Arab Women Artists

1. Lina Ghaibeh
Going Under
1992
Computer generated
photograph
6 1/4 x 9 in.
Collection of the artist

Forces of Change

Salwa Mikdadi Nashashibi
Laura Nader
Etel Adnan

The contemporary art of Arab women reveals a growing self-awareness rooted in admiration, revulsion and resistance— signifying a recognition of the complexities of their history and of the wider world they inhabit. Their art articulates an active resistance to domination and the creation of a new culture, sometimes achieved by exploring and reintegrating layers of history. Using art, Arab women are seizing the moment to make an imprint *upon* the forces of change in their lives. Their art confronts and alters the macro-structures that influence the language, formation of families, and modes of production and consumption in the Middle East— macro-structures that stimulate aesthetic forms celebrating life and mourning destruction.

Exploring Ancient Roots

Artistic expression has been part of the human condition at all times and in all places. As with language, art is a species-centered activity. In the conventions of Euroamerican culture, the arts have become disassociated from the stream of life as artistic creation has increasingly become the function of the specialist. In our definition of art we differentiate "pure" from "folk" art, "fine arts" from "crafts." Such distinctions impede the understanding of art as a basic expression of experience.

Art in the Arab world permeates all ways of life in every country. The living tradition of folk art is seen in the embroidered clothing of brightly draped village women, the Ramadan festival of lights, rug making, pottery decorations, personal adornment and even the designs on foods prepared to celebrate religious rituals and events. Elements of the theater arts are evident in marriage ceremonials, funeral practices and performances of traditional music.

The cultures of North Africa exhibit the greatest continuity in the use of artistic forms. The petroglyphs dating from more than 4000 years B.C. in the Fazzan Valley of Libya and the Tassili petroglyphs in southern Algeria incorporate symbols that still are reproduced on the walls of village homes by women from Algeria's Kabyla tribes who paint with their fingers. In the souks of Damascus one can still buy paintings on glass which visually narrate the age-old folk tales so dear to the people. In Egypt and the Sudan vibrant artforms are created even today by individuals returning from the Hajj who draw the story of their pilgrimage on the outside of their houses, creating images that mix cars and bicycles with camels, palm trees and human figures. Folk motifs also are incorporated in the work of well-known Arab artists. The same folkloric designs that women paint on the storage jars appear in the art of artists such as Rachid Koraichi, Gouider Triki and Baya Mahieddine. Koraichi, a graphic artist from Algeria, employed calligraphy in an abstract, symbolic manner, turning the alphabet into symbols for revolution and protest. Triki's engravings on wood are a subtle synthesis of symbols from contemporary Tunisian culture and traditional imagery from local architecture. Baya, who was born into an age bridging colonialism and modernity in Algeria, bases her dream-like imagery on the Arabo-Berber-Andalusian culture. In her paintings she mixes mysticism, paganism and Islamic ornamentation. In 1947 the renowned French Surrealist André Breton wrote of Baya: **"In a period as the one we are living in, when the Islamic world is scandalously subjected and colonized, Baya's endeavor is significant. Fairy tales are the very heart of a people, and she is a seer, she 'sees,' and she looks to the sky. But she also loves the earth. Flower among flowers, she asks her flowers to nurture those she loves."[1]** The most persistent symbols and signs in this part of the world are those celebrating the cycles of life. Two extremely popular motifs are fish and grape clusters, often rendered not as exact replicas but elaborated with imaginary animals.

Other Arab artists draw inspiration from the vestiges of the region's ancient cultures, combining older iconography with new insights to create fresh artistic expressions. This fusion of elements is evident in the works of several artists who have been influenced by the ancient symbols of Mesopotamia and the rich imagery of Coptic art. Sawsan Amer's works on glass, for instance, combine traditional iconography with personal imagery, mixing the direct frontality of Coptic icons with representations of birds, both real and imagined.

Another artist who joins ancient and contemporary references is Liliane Karnouk from Egypt. "My paintings are in search of a definite cultural union," says the artist. "I belong to a generation trapped between Western and Oriental values."[2] She expresses her search for union by combining tree bark from Canada and the papyrus paper from Egypt in installations such as *Black and Green*, 1992 (plate 3). This work expresses her helpless outrage at the senseless violence of the Gulf War. The black paperworks represent an initial outlet for her mourning for the human and environmental victims of the conflict. The large spatial canvases were conceived as a visual requiem. The tree bark and green seedlings emerge as a source of renewal.

The art of Effat Nagui, a 92-year-old Egyptian artist "who lives in history," draws upon the ancient cultures of northern Africa. One of the pioneers of modern art in Egypt, Nagui was the first woman artist to have a work acquired by the Museum of Modern Art in Cairo, in 1928. Her mixed media works like *Icon of the Nile*, 1991 (plate 4) unite concentric circles and the venerable outline of the mummy with remnants of Coptic parchment and crocodile skins to create contemporary images that utilize the magic of antiquity. As Nagui says:

"Sometimes the artist needs to use materials and forms from ancient and folk art so that he may touch the invisible bases which erected original art. Art is the result of assimilated and inherited culture. I make collage paintings with Arabic manuscripts and I realized that the surface refused to be tackled with gradual colors making illusions. In my 'assemblages' I have collected elements of different sizes of a

2. Sawsan Amer
Icon, 1990
Mixed media on glass
19 x 21 in.
Private collection
Photo by Mark Gulezian

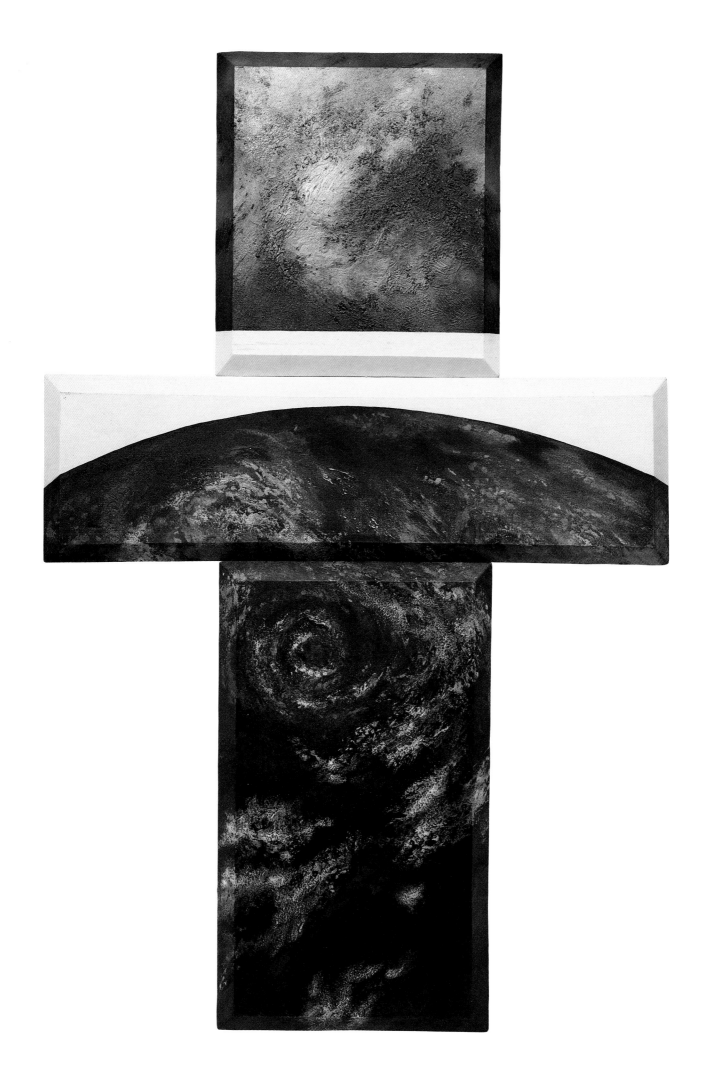

3. Liliane Karnouk
Black & Green
1992
Installation detail
Mixed media on
canvas panel (left)
89 1/4 x 58 in.
Photographic collage
with birch bark and
acrylic (right)
23 x 17 in.
Collection of the artist
Photo by Mark Gulezian

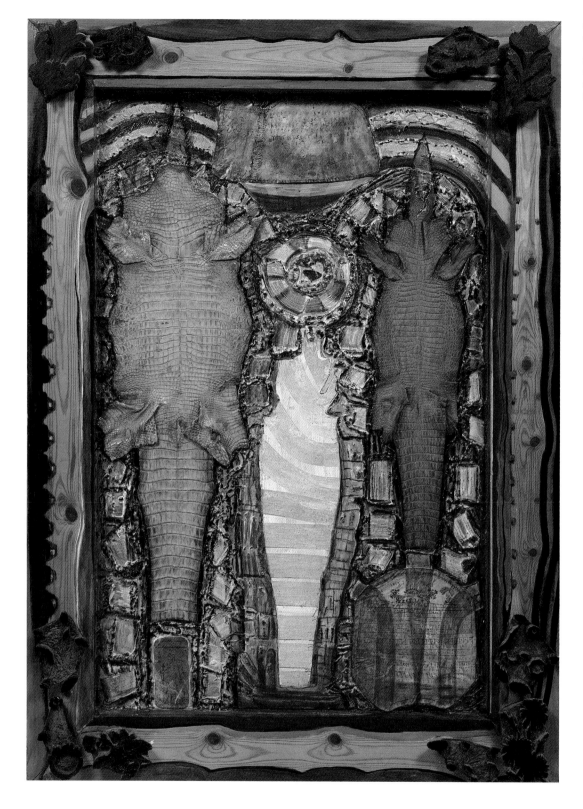

symbolic and spiritual nature forming their own laws on decorative geometric composition. Mixing different elements together is not new—ancient Egyptians did it."³ Nagui's wooden sculptured surfaces, influenced by Nubian architecture, testify to the dynamic and symbolic roles of art forms.

These and other contemporary Arab artists draw inspiration from the past. The Arab East has seen a succession of major civilizations, each creating its own art forms. This is precisely what civilizations are about—creative, centripetal power which fuses old elements with new ideas, giving birth to original and specific new expression.

The Art of Politics

The Arab East has been a battleground in the 19th and 20th centuries. War has been a critical feature of recent history in the region, and wars, per se, create turmoil in a society, accelerating the normal processes of change. Over the past hundred years Arab women have harnessed aspects of the cultural change, transforming their homelands with different degrees of commitment and support.

The French occupation of Egypt in the early part of the 19th century marked a pivotal phase of European influence on the arts of the region. It also initiated a tense dialogue between the West and the East, its tension reflected in the continuing struggle over the regions's heritage, the "authenticity" of its art and its artistic integrity. Todd Porterfield notes that, for Western artists, the Orientalist subject matter often offered easy success as well as new stimuli.⁴ Arab artists, however, found themselves in the middle of the conflicts between the national and international, or even transnational, aspects of art.

The 1919 revolution in Egypt not only fostered a greater sense of nationalism but increased the momentum of the feminist movement developing there since the 1870s. World War I and the fight against colonialism favored the creation of feminist initiatives, such as Huda Sha'rāwī's in Egypt, throughout the Middle East. A leading feminist of her time, Sha'rāwī (ca. 1878–1947) arrived in Cairo from a women's conference in Rome in 1923 and removed her veil at the train station. Just as women led demonstrations, wrote petitions and organized social services that were of vital importance to the impoverished population under British occupation in Egypt, they

played similar roles in nationalist movements in Palestine, Lebanon, Syria, Algeria and other Arab countries struggling against colonialism. World War II stimulated comparable social reactions, and both wars created the need for new labor forces.⁵

During and after the wars women in major cities began working outside the home in offices and factories. Historically, women in the Arab world have worked in agriculture, textiles, carpet weaving and other regional crafts. The opening of schools for women allowed them access to higher education and to public office. Women entered schools of medicine and law, professions which, until then, had been the preserve of men. Women also entered, gradually, and then forcefully, the contemporary art scene.

The art field was one of the first "public jobs" held by women in Egypt, and by the mid-1930s women were active members of the country's modern art movement. Their work had a strong social content. Egyptian artists turned to their national heritage for inspiration. Their art included pharaonic symbols and depictions of peasant life. The work of Egyptian artist Inji Efflatoun exemplifies these trends (plate 17). "My early surrealistic phase ended in 1946 with my complete absorption in feminist, political and social work," she explains. "I began to search for the personality of the Egyptians and the special character of their surrounding environment."⁶

Colonialism, wars, universities established by foreign missions, the cinema and, more recently, the mass media all have affected the cultural models and values of the Middle East. In countries such as Syria, their impact has been resisted. In countries like Lebanon the new models and values have been completely absorbed, becoming nearly indigenous. This has been the process of "modernization."

Over the past two centuries Arabs have been subjugated by foreign rule, a state of affairs that in certain circumstances stimulated Arab self-identity and in others led to subordination and acquiescence. Later, as Arab nationalist feelings peaked under Gamal Abdel Nasser and during the Arab-Israeli wars, Arabs increasingly became participants in events that concerned their physical and cultural survival. This participation accelerated the formation of a national consciousness which mobilized them on every level. This consciousness also functioned as a catalyst for the artists.

One of the first abstract artists in Lebanon and one of the best sculptors in the Arab world is Saloua Raouda Choucair.[7] She recalls that her early commitment to art began as a challenge to her philosophy professor at the American University of Beirut. "He stated that . . . Arabic art is a decorative art of a lower degree, far from being pure art, because the Arabs were not inspired by the nude." Thereupon, Choucair began a lifelong study of Islamic art, exploring its geometry of form and color. Armed with a natural talent for mathematics and physics, along with determination and an inquiring mind, Choucair developed her own abstract style of interlocking shapes as she pursued her research into Islamic art. Through art she was searching for a unity between the spirit of God and her spirit as an artist, the two in one (plate 5). Looking around her she saw this spirit of oneness, unity and infinite repetitiveness in the architecture of the Islamic world. She developed her abstract forms entirely on her own and was surprised, therefore, to find that other artists were working in abstraction when she traveled to Paris in 1948. "I was very excited because there were people there who could understand what I was doing." Nearly fifty years after her exploration of the abstract elements of Islamic art began, Choucair continues to work in the same studio in Beirut using a variety of media—wood, plastic, Plexiglas, metal and stone. She constantly experiments with new materials to create modular forms (some of which are kinetic) that have a mathematical precision. Choucair describes her art as "a form embracing the spirit of Arabesque designs, with their mathematically calculated patterns." She also gains inspiration from Arabic poetry, "which concentrates on the possibility of form."[8]

As the turmoil increased in the region following World War II, women artists began to create more overtly political work. Internal conflicts in Egypt and the rest of the Arab world challenged artists like Inji Efflatoun. A Marxist, she advocated restructuring what she saw as the master-slave relationship between landowners and peasants to alleviate poverty among the peasant class. Her agenda far outdistanced the achievements of Nasser's socialist program. The four years she spent imprisoned because of her political beliefs provided the foundation for a number of paintings.

The euphoria of national liberation in much of the Arab world following World War II gave way before the difficulties each country faced in dealing with many problems simultaneously. Some problems had their seeds in the colonial era and others resulted from the process of modernization. Newly independent countries all over the Middle East struggled to provide basic services in education, health and housing to rapidly growing populations; ensure employment; define the rights and duties of their citizens; and mold the role of women in a manner consonant with the concepts of equality outlined in the United Nations Charter. In addition, they attempted to accomplish all of these political and social goals while preserving their own ancient and valuable traditions.

The conflict over Palestine, which has led to five wars between Israel and the Arab countries since 1948, added another dimension to the Arab struggle for development, directly affecting the progress of the countries involved. The extent to which these social issues have remained unresolved has sharpened the conflicts during the second half of this century.

Such unresolved social problems have engendered protests and stimulated art. Kamala Ibrahim from Sudan draws attention to social inequities through exaggeration and distortion of the female figure (plate 31). Layla Muraywid from Syria, working with layers of handmade paper, earth, cloth, pastel and other mixed media, creates ancient icons in reverence of nature (plate 7). "Life is an accumulation of experience," she says. "Just like my work is a layering of different media, it's never finished." Others, more willing to accept the breakdown of their familiar world, have mastered the art of rehabilitative expression. Baya Mahieddine, steeped in the conflicts of the Algerian Revolution, is simultaneously traditional and transgressive in her work. Filled with bountiful gardens, songbirds, blossoming jasmine and dancing women who are both playful and nurturing, her art combines history and fantasy (plate 21). Her treatment of women links us with the world of pleasure, depicting a freedom that defies patriarchy and Orientalism.

The art of Mounirah Mosly from Saudi Arabia offers the contemplation of high color and gestural energy. Her mural *May You One Day Hear the Crying of a Window Being Born into the World*

5. Saloua Raouda Choucair
Two = One
1947
Oil on cardboard
24 1/2 x 32 in.
Collection of the artist

6. Mounirah Mosly
May You One Day Hear
the Cry of a Window
Being Born into the World
1, 2, 3 and 4
1991-92
Mixed media on tent
fabric with collage
55 x 58 in.
47 x 31 in.
62 ¹/₂ x 60 in.
44 x 38 ¹/₂ in.
Collection of the artist

7. Layla Muraywid
Contemporary Icon 25
1993
Mixed media
26 x 36 1/2 in.
Collection of the artist

is a mixed media collage on tent fabric (plate 6). The artist says it is "meant to reflect a woman's world, memories and vision. The materials were dealt with in a way that empowers them with the strengths of history, geography and the human condition." Mosly says that her approach is like assembling a narrative or composing a sonata. The "chapters" of the narrative include: 1) the net—a place of absolute retreat which describes our active inner lives, a place of dreams, nightmares and the pervasive unconscious; 2) childhood, which recounts a private tale using traditional inks and homemade herbal pigments; 3) the window and the eye which looks through it into the world; and 4) the city, its livelihood, history and archaeology.

Shocked by the intensification of the war in Lebanon and the atrocities to which Palestinians were being subjected, Mona Hatoum, a Palestinian artist from a refugee camp in Lebanon, moved from artist/onlooker to participant. She was drawn into performance art, which became a metaphor for the suffering and struggle of oppressed peoples everywhere. Her art involved the political use of binary opposites, contrasting order and chaos, oppression and resistance as part of a closed system (plate 26). She is a synthesizer of ideas in three-dimensional form. One figure's fall gives rise to another, and vice-versa, revealing the two sides of the same reality: victor/victim, strength/weakness, uniformed/naked.[9]

The Art of Exile
Internal conflicts related to the colonial wars in Lebanon led to civil war in 1975, forcing a large number of artists to live in exile. Ginane Makki Bacho reluctantly left Lebanon in 1984. She describes herself as a storyteller caught between reality and a dream world. Bacho's photographic prints recreate images taken from a diary she kept while she was a "prisoner" of the civil war in Beirut. These experiences have inspired in her the activity of a creator, not the passivity of a mirror (frontispiece). Arriving in New York, Bacho faced continuing social upheavals as she confronted the myths and realities of the New World. She recorded these new experiences as well. Bacho used photography to create a double image of life in Lebanon and life in New York, conveying her experience of being imprisoned in Lebanese shelters during bombing raids and her anguish for a molested child in New York, who is imprisoned in other ways.[10]

Many artists and other Arabs living in exile consider their residency in their respective host countries temporary, something that will last only "until the war is over." Artists seem to visit "home" more often than other professionals, however, continuing to find their inspiration in the Arab world. One Palestinian artist was exiled four times. When we finally contacted her, she refused to loan her artwork. As she explained, she could not part with the few paintings she had been able to preserve, referring to them as "her life."

The same intensity is found in the work and words of Jumana el-Husseini (plate 9). A Palestinian living in Paris, she frequently visits her home in Jericho, where her children cannot go because they carry Saudi Arabian passports. Following an exhibition in Jordan she was asked why she had stopped painting Jerusalem. She answered: **"I haven't stopped painting; I'm still painting in Jerusalem. . . . Before I was painting the houses, the people, the scenes of Jerusalem, but now I'm painting what is under Jerusalem. . . . To me it's like the archaeologist who's brushing the layers of sand each day and what he can find from the days past, from our ancestors. So this really gives me hope. . . . I go back to the earth to see what we had in the past . . . to give me energy, feeling for living."** At another time, when el-Husseini was beginning to create abstract art, she observed, "I'm writing a letter, a letter to our mother who's dead and buried in Jerusalem. . . . This also gives me a connection between life and death, between the living and the dead." El-Husseini incorporates the use of sand in her abstract work. She feels there is force and strength in abstraction. Although her work has evolved from realistic to geometric and abstract styles, el-Husseini has noted that she always paints the same theme—the Arab world and her childhood in Palestine. This recurring subject is somewhat surprising to her since, she says, "outwardly, I'm more Westernized than almost anyone I know."

When Arabs gather, they always talk about passports. El-Husseini, for instance, comments that when she had an Iraqi passport she could not travel anywhere. Her observations on passports, in her art and words, reveal another level of Arab reality. **"From far away you look at this painting and it looks beautiful. And then you look closer and you see the passport and the visas, and you see the ugliness of reality. . . . From a distance, you don't see it, it's only when you come close. You come to look at it and it disturbs you. At the same time, I want it to be pleasing from a distance."**

8. Thuraya al-Baqsami
Cemetery from the East
1989
Watercolor and ink
on paper
19 ¹/₄ x 16 in.
Collection Jordan National
Gallery of Fine Arts
Photo courtesy Jordan National
Gallery of Fine Arts

9. Jumana el-Husseini
Untitled
1991
Mixed media on paper
30 1/2 x 22 1/2 in.
Collection His Royal
Highness Prince Talal
Bin Mohammad

10. Ghada Jamal
Cloud Burst Series 2
1991
Oil on paper
12 1/2 x 14 3/4 in.
Collection of the artist

11. Leila Kawash
Diaspora
1992
Detail
Mixed media collage
on canvas
36 x 30 in.
Collection of the artist
Photo by Mark Gulezian

Several artists were greatly moved by gulf wars of the 1980s and 1990s—a senseless destruction of human life and of thriving urban and rural centers. They also were overwhelmed by the outburst of anti-Arab sentiment that surrounded them in the West, sensing at the same time that their hopes of returning home had diminished. These feelings found their way into their art.

It is interesting to note the gradual development in Ghada Jamal's art from watercolors depicting the poetic serenity of the Lebanese landscape to gouache and oil renditions of the terror of the Lebanese conflict and brutality of the recent Gulf War. Her *Cloud Burst* series (plate 10) consists of aerial landscapes which refer to the early stages of the war, when the blue skies of Iraq were invaded by high-technology warplanes. Circles, arrows and squares mark their layered, earthy patinas, alluding to the charts used for precision bombing. Her abstract landscapes *In the Storm* echo the intensity of violence. The final series, *After the Rains*, reveals the aftermath of war.

Leila Kawash, an Iraqi artist, also speaks of archaeology (plate 11). "Arabs . . . have the advantage of looking way back. We have a very, very strong identity [and feeling of] who we are." Kawash says she explored the early Mesopotamian civilizations "to find something that I'm proud of. I work on layers. . . . I like the archaeology of our land; it's rich, lots of cultures." Her art was affected by the Gulf War as well. **"During the war with Iraq . . . when Americans hit on this shelter [with] a lot of children, and they all ran out and one of them called out "Allah el Akbar" (God is great). And I was painting this painting and when I went back to it, these words, it was like he gathered all the strength—it was like he was combating the whole war with these two words. . . . I spray painted these words and it obliterated all the gold that I was putting on before."**

The Dialogue of Occupation
Growing up during the days of the Algerian Revolution which ended French colonialism, Houria Niati remembers being taken to prison for writing anti-colonial slogans on walls at the age of twelve. This incident led Niati to pursue her work confronting Western Orientalism fifteen years later. Niati states that she started her series *No to Torture* (plates 29 and 30) "because I was dealing with anger." Explaining further she adds: **"Women in Algeria were fighting and dying. They were tortured. Western notions**

of the Oriental imagined a fantasy world of women. Delacroix's Arab women were half naked. The images that he painted were used for many things. Behind his painting [the] suffering, torture, repression, unhappiness and even spiritual happiness was not pictured. Then I started meeting artists around the world painting the same things." Niati lives and works in London. She remembers that, on visiting her first art exhibition in London, she noticed that women were not represented and realized that women's issues were universal.

Laila al-Shawa from Gaza records the harsh realities of Israeli occupation, the Palestinian-Palestinian and Israeli-Palestinian confrontation (plate 12). In an echo of Niati's Algerian struggle, she photographed the graffiti on the walls of Gaza as it appeared before it was obscured by the paint brushes wielded by Israel's occupation army, and the large dollar signs which they used to cover such public expressions. Once the photographs were silkscreened onto canvas, she superimposed geometric designs on them, trying to evoke a sense of order and accentuate the messages. As the basis for other works, she photographed the map of Palestine which had been drawn in red on the sides of cement-filled barricades, confirming an identity which may also seem like a prison to her. Hundreds of such barricades surround the streets of Gaza to prevent the stone-throwing children from escaping. Speaking of her work al-Shawa says, "I recorded a method of communication and punishments which have been sanctified by the 'civilized world.' . . . I have to criticize what is around me through my painting. I don't believe in painting butterflies and flowers and pretty things." Al-Shawa also speaks of the terrible feeling that exists in the Arab world about the West, "a power that is trying to destroy you without ever trying to understand what you are about. Understand that you're a very old culture—that you're a people from a great civilization, that your roots go back thousands of years."

Appreciating Arab Art
It is important not to confuse Arab art with Islamic art. Although Islamic art is still very much alive and is practiced by several artists, it is not the sole basis for contemporary Arab art. Arab artists today draw from an accumulation of sources, the art of Islam being only one of them. Among their many influences are prehistoric art and the art of ancient cultures

12. Laila al-Shawa
Wall of Gaza
1992
Installation detail
Silkscreen
38 x 59 in.
Collection of the artist

13. Madiha Umar
At the Concert
1948
**Ink on white scratch
board**
9 1/2 x 13 in.
Collection Hala Kitani

that developed throughout the Arab world—Egyptian, Sumerian, Byzantine, African.

An Arab today is a citizen of one of twenty states in the Near East and North Africa. Arabs share a history, culture and language. However, the Arab world is diverse, encompassing many ethnic groups, sects, and cultural traits. In addition, the development of contemporary Arab art must be understood within the context of cultural changes taking place for over two centuries.

At least until the 1960s, Western art was considered a fixed paradigm for art in the Arab world. Even within Western art, however, only some artistic currents were privileged. For example, during the middle years of this century abstract Eurocentric art was considered to be the norm, and all other styles and expressions were considered marginal or dismissed categorically. This situation has changed.

The postmodern art of today results from the dislocation of the artistic centers of reference that have held sway for decades in the capitals of the West and the emergence of a multiplicity of centers all over the world. This has led to a restructuring of all pre-1960s concepts, trends, images and styles. What has resulted is the emergence of individual artists working on a global scene.

Arab art often offers few visual clues to its "Arab-ness," partly because the reality of life in the Arab world does not fit preconceptions. For instance, the skyscraper is now a prominent feature of the Kuwaiti skyline. In fact, no major Arab city nowadays presents a cityscape dominated by minarets and domes. Most, if not all, Arab cities, unfortunately, are more "modern" than many European cities which have maintained their ancient monuments and neighborhoods intact. For example, Paris is more old-fashioned than Cairo or Damascus, due to the efficiency of colonial urban planners who wished to wipe out the old features of the Arab world.

The visual environments surrounding Arab artists present enormous diversity and contrast, which is reflected in the works we see. The violence wrought by the forces of change—military, political, cultural—affecting these artists also may be traced in their work, which encompasses not only painting and sculpture but also computer art, performance art, video, collage and more. New ideas, new tools, new forms—we are witnessing the birth of a new age.

The Arab fascination with abstract forms has a significance which extends beyond any depersonalization of the world. To the Arab, geometric and abstract forms represent the *best way* to signify infinity through the conversion of form into pattern. One must be impressed with the fine aesthetics of the geometric designs decorating interiors of village homes in the mountains of Algeria, the exquisite carpets made by Bedouin women in Kuwait and the embroidered patterns of Syrian costumes.

Abstract forms have been incorporated into the modern art movements of Arab countries both in a traditional manner—for their decorative effect—and as a means of advancing nationalistic art. During the 1920s the nationalist art movement in Egypt used a symbol called the *fellaha* (peasant women) to represent the female in Egyptian art. This abstraction incorporated two key concepts, creating a multiplicity of direct and indirect associations: woman (strength and nurturing) and peasant (land and nationalism).[11]

Nowhere has the painted word been used so thoroughly and creatively, both as a link to the past and as a break with that past, as in the Arab world. While some recent Western movements, such as conceptual art, have shown a strong interest in the philosophical and cultural connection between words and images, there has been little artistic emphasis placed on the decorative possibilities of the words themselves, or their visual connection with the past. The use of script, letters or written words, painted on canvases either for their calligraphic value or as integrated figures within a larger surface is, therefore, a distinctive contribution Arab artists have made to contemporary art.

Madiha Umar from Iraq was the first Arab artist to use the Arabic letters in abstract form in 1945. She describes her work as an attempt to free the Arabic letter from its bondage, imprisoned within geometric designs, where it serves simply to fill the space (plate 13). For Umar the letter, like nature, is beautiful in itself. Unlike the calligraphers who intended to show the beauty of the Arabic word, Umar restricted herself to the beauty of the letter.[12]

The word is a very charged symbol in Semitic religions, including Christianity. Islamic

14. Khulood Da'mi
Earth . . . Water . . . Light
1992
Stoneware
10 in. diameter and
12 x 10 ¹/₄ x 2 in.
Collection of the artist

15. Etel Adnan
One Linden Tree,
Then Another . . .
1975
Artist's book, watercolor
and ink on Japanese
paper
10 1/2 x 248 1/4 in. (open)
Collection of the artist
Photo by Said Nousseibeh

culture formalized the word through the writing of the Qur'ān. Some Arab artists use the word as a reference to the spiritual world of Islam, but others are using their own spontaneous handwriting more frequently today in their art to make a secular statement. For instance, Khulood Da'mi from Iraq incorporates poetry in her pottery (plate 14). Perhaps no culture has such a fundamental involvement with the written word as Arab culture.

The Importance of Cross-Influences
Influences have no boundaries and are not one-directional. Art is a domain in which it is easy to demonstrate that, although Western values have left their imprint on other cultures, other cultures have also become part of the fabric of the Western world. The influence we speak of is ongoing.

Many prominent European painters—Eugène Delacroix, Henri Matisse, Paul Klee, Franz Marc, August Macke and Wassily Kandinsky, to name a few—discovered a new aesthetic and a new direction for their work through contact with North Africa. A more current example is Jean Dubuffet's sculptured architectural ensemble created at Périgne called *La Closerie Falballas*. By Dubuffet's own admission we know that the architecture of Mzaab, a Saharan oasis city in southern Algeria, was a major inspiration for this extraordinary artist. The impact of Oriental arts in general, and of Arabic traditions in particular, continues in the arts today.

"I'm going to paint in Arabic"
The Arab world is a "world," not a nation. One can compare it to Oriental music where a single melody can be heard through an infinite number of variations. The Arabic language, with its numerous dialects, patterns of speech and accents, is not always immediately comprehensible to all Arabs. The use of the French language as in North Africa and Lebanon is often a divisive factor. The French-speaking public, for example, often does not read literature published in Arabic. For many writers this situation creates a serious problem, a problem that artists feel they can surmount. Muḥammad Melehi, one of Morocco's greatest artists, has suggested that the large number of Moroccan painters that exists might be explained by the fact that art is a language with no words; in countries where more than one language is being used,

therefore, it can work as a unifying power and have a more immediate and universal appeal. The experience of Etel Adnan seems to support Melehi's theory.

During the Algerian war for independence, many Arab writers who were trained in French because of the colonization of their country faced a crisis. Lebanese artist and poet Etel Adnan says that she was then newly arrived in the United States and had not yet started writing in English. Refusing to write in French as a way of protesting the war, this professor of philosophy and aesthetics told the art faculty of Dominican College of San Rafael in California: "I am going to paint in Arabic!" Adnan proceeded to give artistic form to words by illustrating poetry on long, accordion-like folios (plate 15). As she explored this new form of expression, she concluded that "painting is a language without a language problem."

Artist and singer Houria Niati has found another solution to the barrier caused by language for her, an Algerian living in London. She writes her songs in French, translates them into English and sings in Arabic.

Conclusion
This exhibition of Arab women artists demonstrates that women have become a creative force in the arts. They also have become a creative force in other realms by virtue of their ability to communicate so much that others wish to say but cannot. Many of the pressing issues affecting them resemble women's concerns elsewhere. The strength of their art, however, resides in the fact that it is local—part of their immediate cultural sphere—and also global in its attention to injustice, social inequities, pollution and spirituality. Arab women artists are living in different countries while undergoing similar experiences—political, social, religious and economic.

The steps that Arab women have taken away from well-worn aesthetic paths call for our senses to actively respond. We are long passed the day when ethnocentric notions of art make it necessary to plea for recognition of the art and aesthetics of peoples outside of Europe. Art is not a pristine category of activity untouched by questions of power politics. The art world is decentralizing in the face of global change, and we are all the recipients of new gifts.[13]

Notes

1 André Breton, *Dans le Miroir*, ed. Adrien Maeght (Paris: Galerie Adrien Maeght, 1947).

2 Unless otherwise indicated, this and all subsequent direct quotations from artists are taken from interviews conducted by Salwa Nashashibi during the summer of 1993 and in previous years.

3 Nazli Madkour, *Women and Art in Egypt* (Cairo: State Information Service Press, 1993).

4 Todd B. Porterfield, *Art in the Service of French Imperialism in the Near East, 1798–1848* (Ph.D. thesis: Boston University, 1991).

5 Mona Mikhail, *Images of Arab Women—Fact and Fiction: Essays* (Washington, Three Continents Press, 1979).

6 Madkour, *Women and Art in Egypt*, 37.

7 Helen Khal, *The Woman Artist in Lebanon* (Beirut: Institute for Women's Studies in the Arab World, Beirut University College, 1987), 56.

8 From a letter to Salwa Nashashibi from the artist.

9 Interview with Salwa Nashashibi, summer 1993.

10 Artist's communication with Salwa Nashashibi, 1992.

11 Liliane Karnouk, *Modern Egyptian Art: The Emergence of a National Style* (Cairo: The American University in Cairo Press, 1988).

12 Farouq Yousef, *Madiha Umar and Other Calligraphy*, trans. Hind Kadry-Mathews (Baghdad: University of Literature and Art, Baghdad, 1989).

13 See Thomas McEvilley, "Marginalia: Thomas McEvilley on the Global Issue," *Artforum* 28, no. 7 (March 1990): 19–21.

Women of the Arab World

16. Maisoon Saqr al-Qasimi
*Narration in the Course
of Its Form*
1993
27 1/2 x 19 3/4 in.
Collection of the artist

Turning the Tide

Shehira Doss Davezac

**When they said it was a girl,
the house shook.
It fell on my back.
When they said it was a boy,
I needed no one to lean on.
I stood straight and tall.**

*Song sung in some Egyptian villages
when a child is born*

On February 3, 1993, CNN announced the findings of the United Nations on the status of women. It would take 934 years before women achieved parity with men. Parity has different connotations in different cultures, however.

Like her sisters along the Mediterranean basin, the Arab woman has been expected to marry early, create a family and perpetuate the tradition of promoting the careers of her sons over those of her daughters. How, she has been asking throughout this century, to turn her destiny around? How to have the same rights as a man and still be a woman? How to create an intellectual life and still attain the emotional satisfaction of marriage and children? Must parity, she anxiously wonders, necessitate that same radical act of self-assertion symbolized in the West by Nora Helmer in Henrik Ibsen's *A Doll's House*, who slammed the door of her home behind her? What possibilities are open to her for expressing her political and social views, her dreams for herself and her daughters, her artistic visions?

For an exhibition of Arab women artists such as this to take place in the United States, the girls who metaphorically shook the foundations of their parents' house at birth also have had to shake off social conventions and overcome numerous obstacles. They have confounded expectations of early marriage in favor of a career and have confronted the scarcity of economic and social opportunities open to them. They have challenged their status as women in a man's world and the social restrictions placed on Arab women within an Islamic state that is becoming increasingly militant as the forces of change threaten to undermine its values. They have addressed the political and artistic impact of colonialism. They also have taken advantage of the fast-growing availability of education and employment outside the home.

Additional social and cultural obstacles that they have surmounted include the fact that poetry, music and dance traditionally have had more prestige than painting and sculpture in the Arab world. Class is also a factor—painting and drawing have been accepted accomplishments for girls from upper-class families, but rarely for those from poorer families, who have found it necessary to pursue more lucrative professions.

The paintings in this exhibition tell a story of allegiances and choices involving, among others, gender, religion, economics, politics and education. It is difficult to appreciate the significance of these works without a knowledge of the options that were available to the artists who made them, and the fundamental roles, restrictions or liberties permitted to Arab women.

The Arab woman has had to fight first for her legitimacy in a man's world before fighting for her legitimacy in art. Her predicament was eloquently described in May 1985 by the Egyptian columnist Aḥmad Bahī al-Dīn in the daily *al-Ahrām*: **"Those who interpret the rulings of the Islamic Sharia (law) are men, those who pass laws of all descriptions are men—the world has been a man's world for thousands of years and even if the message of heaven comes to bring women justice,**

17. Inji Efflatoun
Prison **126**
1960
Oil on canvas
11 3/4 x 35 1/4 in.
Collection Gulperie Ismael
Sabry Abdallah
Photo by Mark Gulezian

the world of men listens a little, then goes back to its previous ways."

At its inception, Islamic law was both revolutionary and progressive in according women economic and social rights. Application of the law has been a different matter, however. In the realm of marriage, for example, women often have been coerced into marrying a man of their parent's selection rather than their own, due to familial, economic or social concerns. A 1990 collection of stories by Arab women writers, *Opening the Gates*,[1] deals again and again with the theme of forced marriages. Asserting their right to choose often has required enormous courage for women.

My mother tells of a woman, a high school classmate, whose marriage had been arranged despite her wishes. Having failed to dissuade her parents, she docilely submitted to the elaborate arrangements for the upcoming ceremony. On the day of her wedding, when she was asked before family and friends if she would take this man to be her lawful wedded husband, she said quietly, clearly and without hesitation, "No. And again, no." The marriage did not take place. While she eventually married the man of her choice, her act of defiance always tagged her with the name "Miss No and Again No."

More and more women in the Arab world have started to say "No. And again, no" to what is conventionally expected of them. As Arab women have become more self-consciously assertive, they have increasingly threatened the status quo, however. The fear that Arab women might want to emulate their sisters in the West has prompted religious authorities to mount a campaign asserting the fundamental values of Islamic society and attempting to prove that the status of women in the Arab world is superior to that in the West. As anthropologist Laura Nader has written: **"Knowledge about the West has a strong bearing on the position of women, for it is through this knowledge that the grip on women is justified in many countries of the Middle East. Women are no longer treated as Arab women but as 'potential Westerners,' posing a severe identity crisis. . . . Arab Muslim women resent Western models of aspiration as they encroach on their lives and are used as justification of Moslem 'fundamentalism.'"[2]** Thus the battles waged and won by Western women have become, in some perverse way, an obstacle to Arab women, whose Islamic society is often at odds with Western values.

A history of colonialism in the Middle East has encouraged the association of Western values with Western political domination, fostering nationalist and fundamentalist movements throughout the Arab world. To emulate the West culturally is seen as an act of betrayal, or as evidence of having lost one's roots, traditions and values. In the religious and political climate of the latter part of the 20th century, more and more Arab women artists have questioned the directions that their art should take. Proud of their heritage, these artists ask: How to be liberated and still not model oneself on Western precedent? How to achieve a language of self-expression without borrowing the syllables and sentence-structures of a culture different from our own?

The pull of the West has been even more of a conflict for the many Arab women artists who find themselves living and exhibiting in London, Paris and New York as a result of the wars and the political conflicts that have plagued the Middle East in recent decades. While carrying their cultural heritage with them, their artistic vocabulary is Western and their works develop in directions that parallel those of their sisters in Europe and America. Artists exiled from their countries sometimes have compensated for their exile by plunging the culture they have left behind ever more deeply into their works. The sense of and need for national identity is often more potent in exile than in the country of origin. As Peter Schjeldahl has written on the theme of art and national identity: **"Nationality is one of the most significant and interesting things about anyone, and therefore about any art. It affects the content and character of art at least as much as, say, gender does, even or perhaps especially when an artist tries deliberately to transcend it."[3]**

With the confidence gained by successfully competing in the international arena, some Arab artists, many of whom are living abroad, have now consciously questioned or rejected art forms borrowed from the West. Trained in Western idioms, they have actively sought indigenous artistic styles, rejecting Western art-historical movements as a means of asserting their individuality within the context of a foreign culture. Wasma'a Chorbachi, an Iraqi artist (plate 18), writes of her crises of identity in the 1960s, when her response to a traumatic experience of war in the Middle East took the form of Abstract Expressionism in her paint-

ings. This Western style was the only vocabulary available to her for expressing an Arab experience. She questions the process of art education in the East, by which Arab artists are trained to assimilate Western styles, thus robbing them of a language of forms forged and tempered out of their own culture. Writing about the paintings she produced after the 1967 war she says: **"In looking at my work at that time, I came face to face with a major problem: I suddenly felt that these paintings were not me: 'the Arab and the Muslim.' I realized that this was due to the artistic language or style in which they were painted. . . . They could have been painted by anyone trained in the Western school of contemporary abstract painting . . . . I had not been trained in an artistic language that would enable me to express the inner identity I so strongly felt. . . . I was speaking with a foreign artistic language."[4]**

In the early stages of Arab art movements, to aspire to become an artist was to learn the vocabulary of forms taught by Westerners who were the principal teachers in art schools of the Middle East. The first art schools of the 19th century, such as Egypt's School of Arts and Decoration which opened in 1835, were actually schools of applied art. Their curricula included textile, pottery, wood carving, metalsmithing and carpentry techniques, as well as principles of decoration. It was only in 1908 that a School of Fine Arts, sponsored by a member of the royal family, opened its doors to Egyptian students. The only prerequisite for entrance was talent and the desire to learn.

Despite the Arab world's own many-layered artistic heritage and traditions, the faculty of these early schools consisted of artists from France, England, Italy and Spain who taught the history of Western art beginning with the Renaissance. The students enrolled in these schools were taught to recognize and emulate the different phases of Western art movements. This type of training produced a first generation of modern artists whose works followed the different "isms" of the West: romanticism, neoclassicism, realism, Impressionism, post-Impressionism and symbolism. Gustave Courbet, Vincent van Gogh and Paul Gauguin were among the artists they strove to emulate.

The quest for a national identity in art drove some artists to look closer to home by adapting Mediterranean and ancient Egyptian pharaonic styles to their modern idioms. By the

18. Wasma'a K. Chorbachi
Profession of Faith
1991-92
Ceramic, green glazes
17 in. diameter
Collection of the artist
Photo by Marlene Nelson

19. Samia Zaru
Struggle and Conflict
1985
Oil and collage on canvas
40 x 35³/4 in.
Collection Jordan National
Gallery of Fine Arts

20. Afaf Zurayk
Recollections 13
1993
Mixed media drawing
on paper
8 x 8 1/2 in.
Collection of the artist

1920s these painters and sculptors were called the Pioneer Artists. They were searching for something that Wasma'a Chorbachi had still not found in the 1960s—a language of forms adapted to their own culture. In both material and style, sculptors such as Maḥmūd Mukhtār emulated ancient Egyptian art by using granite, a traditional medium in ancient Egypt, to create monumental statues of contemporary heros who had played a decisive role in the history of colonialism in modern Egypt. Other artists produced paintings of the Egyptian countryside or images of Egyptian men and women working at traditional occupations, recalling ancient Egyptian wall frescos. Mohammad Nagy, a Pioneer painter, created large murals depicting mosque and church, crescent and cross in cityscapes which acknowledged and reinforced symbols of Egypt's religious history.

By 1937, when a group of young Egyptian artists came together under the banner of Surrealism, influences were coming from all directions, but principally from the West. The appeal of Surrealism for Arab artists, both men and women, is not surprising. Intended as a means of expressing the subconscious processes of thought freed from the constraints of reason, it was a style whose approach applied both to literature and painting. Its attraction, therefore, lay partly in the fact that, traditionally, the Arab culture has always been more closely tied to the word than to the image. In addition, it offered a perspective born out of nihilism and despair, which mirrored Arab artists' own sense of political crisis. Finally, it was a style that could free visual artists from the dilemma over issues of cultural identity. Cultural or personal images could legitimately emerge from the nebulous sea of the artists' subconscious, obviating the need to borrow subjects from accepted themes and allowing the personal and the cultural to merge in the same work.

Some of the same characteristics can be seen in the art of Baya Mahieddine, the Algerian artist whose works were praised by André Breton and Pablo Picasso. Her particular poetic stamp imprints the unexplored territory linking the *Thousand and One Nights* to the whimsical logic of *Alice's Adventures in Wonderland*. Her paintings evoke a dream-world, a child's vision of the Garden of Eden—a personal, two-dimensional poetic

vision of the world around her. While the themes and motifs of her village life predominate in her paintings, their richly colorful and rhythmic patterns also remind us of oriental carpets. A self-taught artist, Baya uses traditional motifs from textiles and pottery. Her works have been called a search for "paradise lost." Her great success as an artist—her work can be seen in major museums around the world—is a tribute to her self-taught, indigenous style, which more than compensated for her lack of professional training.

The development of specific artistic styles in the West, such as the Arts and Crafts Movement and Art Nouveau, have validated Arabic art drawn from the folk art traditions prevalent in the Arab world. For instance, Art Nouveau's stylized linear motifs abstracted from nature had strong affinities to the decorative patterns of Islamic art. The infiltration of the Art Nouveau style in the work of trained Arab artists may have helped validate the creativity of their rural counterparts and bridge the gap between work that has customarily been considered "craft" and "art." This may be one explanation for the fact that a new indigenous group of women artists has found legitimacy without Western training in recent decades.

In spite of the greater acceptance of art based on folk traditions in the West, it took an exceptional girl growing up in a rural Arab milieu to see herself as a writer or artist. Coming from a family plagued by poverty and receiving little or no education, she would be expected to defer to the men of the family, marry early and bear many children. Her only access to books would come in preparatory school, once compulsory free education became the norm. Her art education would be through classes in drawing and applied art. She certainly never saw any art in person, except the traditional folk arts and crafts of her village, which were associated with utilitarian objects. If she made it through high school and decided to pursue university training in the arts, she still faced the stigma of being a student in a school of literature or art. The majority of those studying literature or art had received such low test scores that they were not admitted to the professional schools that would prepare them for more lucrative careers in medicine, law, agriculture, engineering or architecture. Only a small number of students in the arts were there out of choice—because

21. Baya
Femmes Portant
de Coupes
1966
Gouache on paper
39 ¹/₂ x 59 in.
Collection L'Institut
du Monde Arabe
Photo by Maillard

they excelled in the field and were propelled by their talent and strength of character to make a career in the creative arts.

Nawāl al-Sa'dāwī, the famous Egyptian feminist and writer, and Chaibia Tallal, a Moroccan painter of international renown, personify the character and dedication required to succeed as an artist from a rural background. Chaibia comes from a poor, agricultural, illiterate family. Against all odds, she carved out a distinctive creative identity (plate 22). In an interview, Chaibia remembers: **"At fifteen, I was widowed. I was a peasant. I was illiterate. You must understand, it's important not being afraid to be different. You must know the rest, otherwise you would not understand my success. You have to know that when I was little I used to do unusual things. I used to make flower crowns and wear them on my head. Nobody ever did that. They thought I was mad."**[5]

It was easier for a poor, rural girl to aspire to become a writer than to become an artist because tradition allowed for it. Etel Adnan, a writer who also happens to be a painter included in the current exhibition (plate 15), comments: **"In Arab countries, society does not like women in politics, but does respect women writers. There is such reverence for literature in the Arab world and such love for poetry, that even women share in that respect. They are not censored because they are women."**[6] As potential writers, women forced into positions of deference could listen to conversations in which they were not asked to participate. They could observe, record, protest or plot silently in their diaries and could release their anger with imagined written scenarios that recorded their pain or happier emotions. All this could be done at home, secretly, silently, without threatening or disturbing the status quo.

Such Western researchers as Miriam Cooke express their surprise at the strength and extent of writings by Arab women. Long before the American author Kate Chopin wrote her novel *The Awakening* in 1899, which caused great controversy because of her explicit treatment of female sexuality, women from Egypt, Lebanon and Syria, Cooke asserts, were "writing literature that was far from being docile . . . was often covertly subversive, even volcanic, and almost profoundly revisionary."[7] By the early 20th century Arab women writers held salons and gathered around them the intellectuals of the day. Mayy Ziādah (1886–1941) exemplifies these

women. A Lebanese Christian, she went to Egypt in 1908. As a writer of poetry, short stories, essays and plays, she was respected by the intellectual circles of her time. She was highly influential, and her literary salon was open to intellectuals of many Arab and European nationalities.

A recent exhibition in the College Library at Harvard University arranged by Alice C. Deyab displayed the magazines which Arab women have published for almost one hundred years.[8] Today there are over three hundred magazines published by women. Even before World War I, there were more than twenty-five feminist Arab journals owned, edited and published by women in Cairo, Beirut, Damascus and, to a lesser extent, Baghdad. In one such journal, *al-Fatāt* (Young girls), published in Egypt in 1892, Hind Nawfal, its creator and editor, writes: **"Al-Fatāt is the only journal for women in the East; it expresses their thoughts, discloses their inner minds, fights for their rights, searches for their literature and science, and takes pride in publishing the products of their pens."**[9]

It is revealing that in enumerating the fields which concern women, Nawfal cites literature, science and "the products of their pens" but not the products of their paint brushes or chisels. Indeed, the visual arts have had a different history than literature. Both in the East and in the West, art was long considered the domain of men. Although women poets were celebrated for their elegies as early as the pre-Islamic and Umayyad periods, no names of Arab women artists from those periods have come down to us. Pliny does cite Helen of Egypt, a painter working during the 2nd century B.C., however, among the few names of women artists in antiquity that he mentions. While today feminist art historians in the West have unearthed the names of neglected women artists who were famous during their own lifetimes, no comparable names to those of Artemisia Gentileschi, Lavinia Fontana and Sofonisba Anguissola, to name a few, have ever appeared in the Arab world.

To be taken seriously as an artist has been particularly difficult for women from the Arab region. As the Lebanese-Armenian artist Seta Manoukian (plate 25) writes: **"The problem of a woman artist is a difficult one. In her independence, in freeing herself of all conventional attitudes, she ceases to perform conventionally as a woman; she**

22. Chaibia
Village de Chtouka
1982
Oil on canvas
71 x 71 in.
Collection L'Institut
du Monde Arabe
Photo by Maillard

23. Amna Abdalla
Untitled
1992
Batik on silk
7 1/2 x 7 in.
Collection of the artist

24. Maysaloon Faraj
Sisters in Black and Gold
1988
Stoneware
21¹/₂ x 11 in.
Collection Raya Jallad

25. Seta Manoukian
Willing to Begin
1990
Acrylic on canvas
82 x 70 in.
Collection of the artist

26. Mona Hatoum
Untitled
1992
Wire mesh
38 1/4 x 17 1/2 x 28 in.
Collection of the artist
Photo by Edward Woodman

insists on being a person, and, on a human level, no different than a man. The problem is that men keep regarding her just as a woman, and expect her to act in conformity with their pre-conceived image of a woman."[10] The Palestinian painter Jumana el-Husseini feels women artists who wish to be taken seriously need to work harder to prove themselves. She adds: "People have the idea that women are changeable creatures, not serious, that a woman takes up painting out of boredom—tries her hand at it for a while and then turns her interest elsewhere. They question whether a woman's work is worth investing in—maybe she won't be painting in ten years . . . then what will her painting be worth? They refuse to believe that a woman can be a genuine artist, that she can be as totally dedicated to her art as a man."[11]

This is the centuries-old problem that women artists, both in the East and the West, have typically had to face. In his *De claris mulieribus* (On famous women), the 14th-century writer Giovanni Boccaccio names only three women painters from antiquity whom he introduces as proposed models for women painters of his own time, with this proviso: "I thought that these achievements were worthy of some praise, for art is very much alien to the mind of woman, and these things cannot be accomplished without a great deal of talent, which in women is usually very scarce."[12] In the 16th century Giorgio Vasari praised women artists for their "grace, industry, beauty, modesty and excellence of character" but never for their genius. He effectively set the art history canon for judging the works of women artists for future generations, and his view of the matter has not radically changed even in the 20th century.

It took pioneer art historians, such as Linda Nochlin in the early 1970s, to question traditional assessments of women's art. In posing the question "Why have there been no great women artists?", Nochlin argues: "A *feminist* critique of the discipline is needed which can pierce cultural-ideological limitations, to reveal biases and inadequacies not merely in regard to the question of women artists, but in the formulation of the crucial questions of the discipline as a whole."[13] Although Arab women artists are slowly gaining recognition in their own countries and a few male voices can now be heard speaking on their behalf, a feminist critique of Arab art is still very much in the future.

Another difficulty which confronts Arab women artists and poses a dilemma is the marketability of their work, alluded to previously by el-Husseini. Much of the demand for art comes from patrons unschooled in contemporary Western art whose taste runs to the familiar rather than the innovative. Such patrons favor works with traditional motifs and local themes. Access to international artistic forums, however, often depends upon the use of an internationally recognized language of form and content for which there is neither demand nor understanding in the Arab world. This dilemma faced by Arab artists is made even more acute by the very nature of the national identity crisis which some artists experience.

In the works of Arab women artists shown in this exhibition, we find a variety of styles and preoccupations, ranging from traditional, indigenous and local viewpoints to others that reflect very new and innovative approaches. Many have chosen the language of international culture or "cosmopolitan culture" as defined by Peter Schjeldahl: **"In culture, the alternative to the national is not the universal. It is the cosmopolitan, a sophisticated mingling and cross-pollination of national qualities. It has always been thus, even in heydays of Internationalism. Maleviich, Mondrian and Pollock were, respectively, as Russian, Dutch and North American as vodka, windmills and quarter horses."[14]**

In their work Arab women artists have experimented with a variety of different media. The computer images of Samia Halaby and the installations of Mona Hatoum give some idea of the range. While both Halaby and Hatoum are conscious of their origins, they still see themselves not as members of a particular region, race or gender, but as artists pursuing the serious causes of art itself. Some of the artists have lent their voices to the growing international ecological movement. One example is Liliane Karnouk, whose installations denounce the carnage caused by oil spills and industrial waste (plate 3). A number of artists in the show produce art that is closer to what one might call naive or folk art. Such is the work on glass of the Egyptian artist Sawsan Amer (plate 2). Her rich color sense may come from Egypt's own love of vibrant, resonating colors, or may result from a conscious awareness and application of Fauve innovations, learned through her study of Western art and adapted to local themes. Other artists, having found an affinity between Western abstract movements and Islamic artistic traditions, have incorporated the stylized abstractions of Islamic calligraphy into works that echo

Abstract Expressionist techniques. An example of this approach is seen in the art of Wijdan Ali (plate 43). Abstract Expressionism itself, like Surrealism before it, has captured the interest of many of these contemporary painters. It would seem as if this style permitted an artist, caught in a dilemma over stylistic approaches, to find a means of expression which, while accommodating the personal, is still within the canon of modern art. Yet others have developed a style singularly their own. Zeinab Abdel Hamid's scenes of old Cairo streets incorporate a multiplicity of skewed lines and angled perspectives to convey a sense of the city's compressed energy and crowded spaces. Obliquely political, the works of the Palestinian artist Vera Tamari are like palimpsests, evoking layer upon layer of political history. In pieces such as *Rhythms of the Past*, 1993 (plate 27), she superimposes ancient ceramic shards dug up from the soil of historic Palestine on scenes abstracted from the present. The same layering of meaning permeates the work of Leila Kawash (plate 11). Her abstract paintings reveal, as we look closer, different passport entry-stamps, symbols of her own and of her compatriots' refugee status and ongoing displacements from country to country.

As this exhibition demonstrates, the problems that Arab women artists confront have had many solutions. Like artists the world over, each woman artist whose work is on display has made a conscious choice concerning the directions that her art must take—cosmopolitan or nationalistic, political or apolitical, religious or secular. Whatever direction these Arab women artists have chosen, it is significant that they have said "No. And again, no" to their predicament. They have done so as women, as Arabs and as artists.

Today women in the Arab world indeed have slammed the door on their traditional roles and stepped out into the world of politics, economics, business, medicine, art. They are now members of parliament, owners of their own businesses, directors of museums, professors in universities. They are published writers and exhibited artists whose works travel the museum and gallery circuit in Europe and now in America with this exhibition of their art. In saying "no" to the restrictive dictates that could have circumscribed their ability to produce the paintings reproduced here, these women have said "Yes. And again, yes" to their creative visions.

27. Vera Tamari
Rhythms of the Past
1993
Ceramic
9 1/2 x 6 in
Collection of the artist

28. Samia Halaby
Variable Motion
1993
Oil on canvas
36 x 46 in.
Collection of the artist

Notes

1 Margot Badran and Miriam Cooke, eds., *Opening the Gates: A Century of Arab Feminist Writing* (Bloomington, Ind.: Indiana University Press, 1990).

2 Laura Nader, "Orientalism, Occidentalism and the Control of Women, *Cultural Dynamics* 2, no. 3 (1989): 327.

3 Peter Schjeldahl, "Art & National Identity: A Critics' Symposium," *Art in America* 79, no. 9 (September 1991): 80.

4 Wasma'a Khalid Chorbachi, "Arab Art Twenty Years Later," *ASQ* 11, nos. 2 and 3 (Spring/Summer 1989): 144.

5 From an interview of the artist conducted in Casablanca by Fāṭima Mernissī, January 1985.

6 Hillary Kilpatrick, "An Interview with Etel Adnan," in *Unheard Words: Women and Literature in Africa, The Arab World, Asia, The Caribbean and Latin America*, ed. Mineke Schipper and trans. Barbara Potter Fasting (London and New York: Allison and Busby, 1985), 117.

7 Miriam Cooke, "Telling Their Lives: A Hundred Years of Arab Women's Writings," *World Literature Today* 60 (Winter 1986): 212.

8 *Harvard University Library Notes*, March 24, 1988.

9 Bouthaina Shaaban, "The Hidden History of Arab Feminism," *Ms.* 3, no. 6 (May/June 1993): 76.

10 See Helen Khal's interview with Seta Manoukian in *The Woman Artist in Lebanon* (Beirut: University College, Women's Studies in the Arab World, 1987).

11 Khal's interview with Jumana el-Husseini in *The Woman Artist in Lebanon*.

12 Giovanni Boccaccio, *Concerning Famous Women*, trans. and intro. Guido Guarino (New Brunswick, N.J.: Rutgers University Press, 1963), 132.

13 Linda Nochlin, "Why Have There Been No Great Women Artists?" in *Art and Sexual Politics*, Elizabeth Baker and Thomas B. Hess, eds. (New York: MacMillan, 1973), 2.

14 Schjeldahl, "Art & National Identity," *Art in America* (September 1991): 80.

Western Views
of Oriental Women

29. Houria Niati
No to Torture
1982-93
Installation detail
(1982–83)
71 1/2 x 108 1/2 in.
Collection of the artist

in Modern Painting and Photography

Todd B. Porterfield

Since their invention two centuries ago, museums and galleries in Europe and the United States have presented little in the way of works by contemporary Arab women artists, yet they have purveyed a great deal of Orientalism, art by Westerners (usually men) about the East. Europe in the 19th century was positively awash with images of "Oriental" women. Not coincidentally, representations of Eastern women constitute a subject with which Western audiences seem unusually well-informed: Recall the Gulf War and the mileage wrought from the question of Saudi women, veiled and driving cars, or forbidden to drive at all. Did any report on daily Arab life elicit so much attention, so much certain response, about the relative merit of Arab life compared to that of the West?

The huge number of images of Oriental women has long been accepted as the most characteristic part of an even larger number of Orientalist pictures. The profusion of this category of picture has been traced to the development of the museum and gallery system, the increased frequency of artists' traveling to the East and the advancement of modern Western imperialism. Until very recently, Western audiences viewed Orientalist pictures as authentic representations by the artist of his Eastern subjects. In the traditional account of Orientalism, the strange and novel experience of the dazzling light, bizarre customs and weird physiognomies of the East compel the artist to leave his own culture aside and simply document what is before him.[1]

Recent scholarship has revealed problems with unanalytical approaches that accept pictures as simply unalloyed, two-dimensional copies of the "Orient." Edward Said and Linda Nochlin have argued that Orientalism, in whatever field, does not stand as proof of

dialogue between East and West. They demonstrate how Orientalism is a discourse—an internally coherent and delimited, fantasy-based description of the Orient which has served to rationalize and advance Western imperialism in the very real and geographic East.[2] Now the question of the meaning and function of Orientalist art is rich, and the stakes are high.

To apprehend the dynamics and purpose of Orientalist art, we must examine images of Eastern women in light of fundamental trends in Western picturemaking of which Orientalism partakes: the illustrated travel account, naturalist painting, photographic documentation and modernist abstraction. This is how Orientalist pictures carry meaning—through their relation to other pictures and conventions in the Western tradition. Moreover, to demonstrate the cultural and political work done by Western views of Oriental women, we will have to offer readings of specific images as they pertain to specific events in the periods of conquest, colonization, revolution and post-colonialism. Our brief overview of the meaning and application of this cultural production necessitates a long but narrow scope. One approach suggested by the works in this exhibition concerns works made in France about its North African colonies. We should begin by examining at some length the painting that has often been placed at the beginning of the modern Orientalist tradition.

Eugène Delacroix's *Women of Algiers* (Les Femmes d'Alger dans leur appartement, fig. 1) is often considered a foundation stone in the edifice of modern Orientalist painting. It has long been accepted as an eyewitness account of the most characteristic Orientalist subject—the Muslim harem—based on the artist's 1832 trip to North Africa. While divided by a variety of political and aesthetic allegiances, critics of the painting's inaugural exhibition at the 1834 Paris Salon could agree on one thing: Delacroix's work was scientific. His advocates praised this attribute, and his detractors lamented it.[3] One complained that the painting had too much reality, "too much of these voluptuous and lazy creatures."[4] All agreed, however, that it was real and true. Over the years its reputation has continued to be construed as scientific, actually ethnographic, in its ostensibly scrupulous portrayal of the physiognomies, mores, costumes and living conditions of an exotic people. In the 1880s, for instance, the realist critic Philippe Burty placed the *Women of Algiers* first in what he called "the modern ethnographic school."[5] In the 1930s, as if to corroborate this assessment of the previous century, the Musée Ethnographique du Bardo in Algiers displayed a three-dimensional recreation of Delacroix's painting.[6]

The creation and application of ethnography go to the core of Delacroix's picture and the Orientalist enterprise. It was in 1831, the year of Delacroix's departure for Algiers, that the term *ethnographie* was coined—meaning a study of the distinction between human races by the understanding of idioms, physiognomies and social status. It was seen as a step toward the gradual diffusion of European civilization. This new science was consecrated in the foundation of Paris's Musée Ethnographique in 1831. Its curator defined its mission: to know "in an exact and positive (scientific) manner the degree of civilization of the peoples barely advanced on the social ladder," with the expectation that science and commerce should benefit from Africa's opening by the conquest of Algiers, now a "place of power of the French army."[7] Delacroix created his *Women of Algiers* not only in the same years, but also with the same assumptions about scientific observation and the relative merits of French and Algerian life. Like ethnography itself, Delacroix's picture was created and exhibited neither in a scientific laboratory nor in a vacuum. To say that he went to the Near East as a disinterested artist-scientist would be to overlook the circumstances of his voyage.

In 1831 the Comte de Mornay invited Delacroix to join him on a diplomatic mission to Morocco, Spain and Algeria. Mornay was sent by the government of France's constitutional monarch, Louis-Philippe, to secure Moroccan cooperation in the completion of France's conquest of Algeria.[8] By inviting Delacroix, Mornay had in his company an artist who, while having never left Europe, had already created a formidable Orientalist oeuvre, associating Orientals with violence and licentiousness, and advocating the cause of the Greeks in their war for independence against the Ottoman Empire. Delacroix's job, it seems, was to produce a painting celebrating the accord with Morocco.

While Mornay failed to secure the treaty, Delacroix succeeded in other venues, thanks to the French military presence in Algeria. During his three-day stay in Algiers, Delacroix gained access to a Muslim harem through the intervention of a certain Poirel, who administered the port of the French-occupied city. Thus, due to his country's dominant political position, Delacroix was able to violate Muslim rule, an offense which is the enabling conceit behind his painting of 1834. Reports of Delacroix's visit to the harem state that it was his hope, expectation and "strongest desire to get in a Muslim interior which was severely forbidden to Christians."[9]

The expectations and desires Delacroix brought to his first real encounter with the Orient were indebted to his extensive experience of the East through Orientalist literature and imagery produced in the West. For the armchair connoisseur of the ethnicity, toilette, costume and sexuality of Oriental women, to enter a Muslim harem of Algerian women was especially desirable: **"The women of Algiers are, according to the Orientals, the prettiest from the Barbary coast. They know how to complement their beauty with rich silk fabrics and velvets, embroidered in gold. Their complexion is remarkably white. If their hair is blond, they dye it black, and those who already have that nuance are dyed with a henna preparation. Natural flowers, roses and jasmine ordinarily accompany their elegant hair."[10]** In fact, Delacroix so hotly anticipated the encounter that, although he later reported that what he saw was not erotic, even his physical response was guided by his Orientalist learning. An associate reported that he "spent a day, then another in this harem, a prey to an exaltation which translated itself into a fever which was hardly calmed by sherbet and fruits."[11]

Delacroix's public—including critics and historians—has greatly mythologized the artist's "penetration" of the harem. One of Delacroix's associates imagined what must

have been going through the artist's mind:
"When, after having crossed through some dark hall-
way, one penetrates the part which is reserved for
them; the eye is truly dazzled by the sparkling light,
by the fresh faces of women and children, appearing
suddenly in the midst of this mass of silk and gold.
For a painter there is a moment of fascination and of
strange happiness. That must have been the impres-
sion felt by Delacroix and it is that he transmitted to
us in his painting the *Women of Algiers*."[12]

Delacroix's painting is large and ambitious.
The figures are placed logically in the imaginary space of the harem. Three women sit in
the low, cramped interior. They are gathered
in a circle around a water pipe, leaving space
and access for the viewer. Light floods in from
the upper left, illuminating the costumes,
objects, habits and physiognomies. The play
of light in the foreground is contrasted against
the deep shadows of the back of the room,
which correspond to the sultry demeanor of
the harem women and their smoky gazes. The
whole scene is made accessible by the striding
black slave who pulls back the curtain on the
women of Algiers. Yet, despite the claims of a
century of Orientalist studies, the curtain has
not been pulled back to reveal an authentic

and objective image of Delacroix's dialogue
with the East. Rather, it is drawn apart to
reveal Delacroix's "knowledge" about the
Orient, knowledge acquired before his departure, part of a larger culture of Orientalism
contrived in the West and serving its purposes.

Delacroix's experience of the harem and his
audience's experience of his painting were
highly mediated. Among the many illustrated
accounts of the East that Delacroix knew
before his trip was Rosset's *Moeurs et Coutumes
Turques et Orientales: dessinés dans le pays en 1790*
(Paris, Bibliothèque Nationale). Delacroix's
general approach to sketching on the trip followed a formula found in Rosset and elsewhere—the artist used watercolor, gave specific description of costume and rendered a
highly palpable atmosphere. He repeated
Rosset's iconographic concerns in his sketches
of city views, costume studies, portraits and
scenes of daily life. Moreover, the three seated
figures in his *Women of Algiers* closely resemble
the figural groupings in Rosset's harem scene,
Turc avec ses femmes (Turk with His Wives).
The four figures in *Women of Algiers* all have
links to illustrated travel accounts of the
East and to the tradition of Western painting.

Figure 1. Eugène Delacroix, *Women of Algiers*, 1834. Oil on canvas, 71 × 91 in. Musée de Louvre, Paris

30. Houria Niati
No to Torture
1982-93
Installation detail (1993)
41 1/2 x 35 1/2 in.
Collection of the artist

This is to say that Delacroix's previous indoctrination and practice in the culture of Orientalism informed his project. Before going to the Orient, he knew how to paint it.

Delacroix's public at the Salon of 1834 was equally sure about what it saw. How, after all, could critics proclaim Delacroix's picture authentic without ever having gone to Algiers? The Orientalist painter and sometime critic Alexandre-Gabriel Decamps wrote that the poses "of these Africans [have] a sentiment of indolence," and the beauty of the heads "expresses all the insipidity and inaction of these ignorant minds of the Levant."[13] The "truth" which Decamps and his cohorts recognized in the painting of 1834 served as an index of the social corruption and the political decline of the Orient. The critic Gabriel Laviron expresses the prevailing sentiments of the day: **"In seeing this picture, one really understands the boring life of these women who do not have a serious idea, nor a useful occupation to distract themselves from the eternal monotony of this prison in which they are enclosed."[14]**

While passing for scientific, Delacroix's painting elicited a long-standing refrain about the harem. It evoked both desire for the women and repulsion at the Orient's inferior social and political systems. Most striking is the comment by the critic Gustave Planche, who, like all the other commentators, repeated clichés about the harem, seeing the figures full of "sluggishness and nonchalance." While proclaiming that Delacroix's rendition was truthful, he thanked the artist for omitting the women's dirty fingernails.[15] Thus, even if Delacroix had attempted to paint a sympathetic picture of an Oriental subject by, for instance, insisting on the women's cleanliness, it would not have mattered to his public. The critics' previously informed knowledge about the Orient stepped in to insure the invocation of the Orientalist discourse.

With the exhibition of Delacroix's *Women of Algiers*, the style, subject, purpose and reputation for authenticity of the illustrated travel account—one source of all this Orientalist knowledge—were brought to the realm of high art. In addition to the influence of Rosset's work on Delacroix's ideas, we can look to Antoine-Ignace Melling's 1819 *Voyage pittoresque de Constantinople et des rives du Bosphore*, another book which the artist consulted before his departure.[16] In one of his four plates devoted to the sultan's harem, Melling provides an architectural cutaway diagraming the interior and its workings (fig. 2). This distant and objectifying viewpoint helps authenticate the picture and invites the reader to "penetrate" the harem. While Delacroix's technique is more sensual and colorist than linear and painstaking, both images serve up access to the harem in naturalizing, information-conveying styles. The moralizing posture associated with objective views of the harem is made clear in Melling's text. The harem, which he so scrupulously details in pictures, signifies the lubricity of Oriental societies, their "denatured law" and the hazards of lesbian love.[17] Finally, both Melling's and Delacroix's works imply the politically superior position of the picturemaker over his subject.

Melling's unprecedented access to the royal harem is attributed to his enlightened science, to his practice as a physician, which he opposes to the backwardness and innate tyranny of the rulers of the Ottoman Empire, "now crumbling under the weight of its vices."[18] In both harem scenes the implied science and objectivity of the Western author stand in contrast to the depravity of the social structures represented. Delacroix's painting is essential to the history of Western images of Oriental women because it establishes a paradigm of function and purpose that is viable well into the 20th century—presenting a contrived reality to satisfy preconceived expectations. *Women of Algiers* passes for one thing, in this case, objective or scientific fact, while it provokes a long-standing, moralizing cant about the depravity of the East. The artist's access to his subject signals his superior political position, which both derives from and fuels the imperial enterprise.

The immediate political context of Delacroix's painting is revealed in its relation to the substantial imagery which depicted France's 1830 conquest of Algeria. Printmakers had quickly equated the invasion of Algiers to the penetration of the Muslim harem and the possession or rape of its women. One print depicts French soldiers raping Algerian women—*Les Fruits de Victoire* (Fruits of Their Victory), the title says.[19] In image after image the triumphant French soldiers enter the great harem and cart off and rape the favorite of the ruler. Even the nincompoop Jean-Jean, a French version of Sad Sack, is rewarded with a woman simply because he is a French soldier.[20]

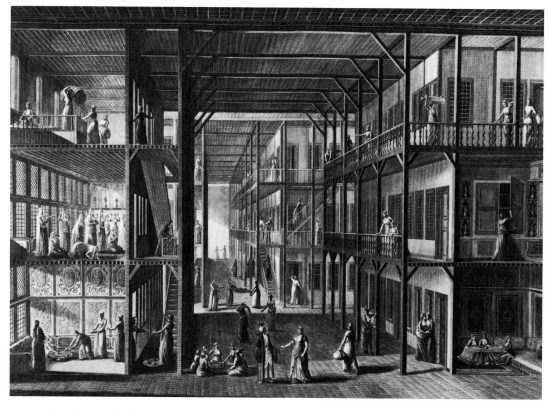

Figure 2. Antoine-Ignace Melling, *Intérieur d'une partie du HAREM du Grand-Seigneur*, engraving from *Voyage pittoresque de Constantinople et des rives du Bosphore*, 1819. Bibliothèque Nationale, Paris

Delacroix and the makers of more plebeian images had provided a currency which supported the imperial policy and which proved highly flexible. The 1830 images of rape celebrated the conquest of Algiers, and Delacroix's painting coincided with the French government's decision to colonize its "African possessions."[21] Ten years later a lithograph called *Un Bonheur Oriental* (An Oriental Delight) appeared.[22] It depicts a French soldier sitting down to a hookah with "the charming Aicha." Their postures and the setting recall Delacroix's 1834 Salon painting. The soldier feigns sexual passivity, telling the harem woman: "I am available for your use . . . I had at first the intention to French you but I find it really sweeter for you to Bedouinise me!" Tastefully kept out of the frame of Delacroix's painting, the French military presence materializes here, just in time to celebrate the French victory at Isly (Morocco). Whether it was Melling in Constantinople, Delacroix in Algiers or the *Oriental Delight* in the context of Morocco, the ideology was the same. It continued to rationalize the imperial cause.

Later in the 19th century imperial expansion, tourism and the reproductive picturemaking industry flooded Europe with photographs, postcards and prints of Oriental scenes which

followed Delacroix's example. The market for these images proved lucrative. Already by 1876 France's Bonfils family not only had a studio in Beirut but a mail-order business as well.[23] Postcards like the *Cracked Jug* (fig. 3) presented the Oriental woman bare-breasted, frankly and amiably addressing the viewer. The postcard employs a convention made most famous in Jean-Baptiste Greuze's 1780 painting, *The Broken Pitcher* (Paris, Musée du Louvre), in which the artist indicates that the jug is cracked, ruined. Greuze's bedraggled girl, tattered, post-coital and clutching a broken pitcher, is meant to titillate the viewer and blithely teach a lesson on sexual virtue. In the postcard, on the other hand, the vessel is pristine; what is broken is the sexually (and continually) available Oriental woman.

While relying on the high art tradition of Greuze and Delacroix, the *Cracked Jug* functions on other levels as well. The photographer is anonymous. His picture is numbered and titled—*6596 SCÈNES ET TYPES*—suggesting that this figure is one specimen among many. The creation and marketing of the postcard operate in a more frankly commercial vein than the Salon painting. Once purchased in the East, the card becomes a personal message carrier, and the messages are typically banal, having nothing to do with the content of the image, except in the most important geopolitical way—the sender is in the East as a result of Western power, and the image conveys the corruption of its people, which justifies the imperial presence.[24] While one side of the card may comment on the weather, the other visually reminds the correspondents of the rationale and purpose of their political role in the world. As if this contrast were not strong enough, the postcard's stamp makes it clear. The "République Française" is represented by the striding, idealized, Greco-Roman-inspired figure of Marianne, wearing the Phrygian bonnet, symbol of the freed slave and the French Revolution—the antithesis of the fleshy, erotic, earthy, available and completely real (we are told) Oriental woman. This conjunction of Marianne and the Oriental nude brings together the symbol of the, ostensibly, liberty-loving French with the symbolism of the despotism inherent in Oriental self-rule. Imperialism is justified, and the correspondents can go about their business.

The tradition of true, or modern, Orientalism is usually said to end a century after Delacroix's *Women of Algiers*. A figure like Henri Matisse is seen as making frankly undocumentary pictures, interested in Oriental

Figure 3. *6596 SCÈNES ET TYPES—La Cruche fêlée—LE.* Postcard from Malek Alloula, *The Colonial Harem.* Collection of Malek Alloula

subjects only as a pretext for his investigations into Painting. While it may be fair to think that Matisse was trying only to replicate familiar motifs in a personal and innovative style, his works, too, functioned in ways beyond the aesthetic. He might have hoped that his pictures were strictly escapist, aesthetic fantasies, that they operated out of the realm of quotidian political concerns, but his depictions of Oriental women are patent proof of the impossibility of such a project.[25]

Matisse was devoted to the Orient early in his career, visiting Munich in 1910 to see a major Islamic art exhibition, traveling to Algeria in 1906 and to Morocco in the winters of 1911–12 and 1912–13. His works from Morocco combine a typical litany of Orientalist subjects with his most important abstract innovations in painting. These aspects are found to a lesser extent in works made well after his Oriental excursion, such as his *Odalisque in Red Trousers* of 1921–22 (fig. 4). In the decor around the central figure we see the fruits of Matisse's Fauvism of the first decade of the century: unmodeled expanses of vibrant color and flat patterning. Yet, the subject and the classical draftsmanship used in rendering the volumetric torso of the reclining nude recall the grand tradition in painting, from Titian to Delacroix, to Ingres and Renoir. Matisse's stylistic synthesis makes the subject of the Oriental woman modern, acceptable and august.

The strategy paid off. *Odalisque in Red Trousers* was the first Matisse purchased by the French government for a Parisian museum. Léonce Bénédite, curator of the Luxembourg Museum and president of the Society of Orientalist Painters, made the acquisition. In a tamed-down modernist language, Matisse had updated the discourse about Oriental women in time to help celebrate France's extension of its empire during World War I. The purchase of the painting preceded by just three weeks the opening of the massive Exposition Coloniale (April—November 1922), intended to glorify, justify and expand the French empire.[26]

Odalisque in Red Trousers also succeeded by contributing to a general backlash against modernist abstraction, including Fauvism, which Matisse himself had helped to invent. This "return to order" meant the official marginalization of work that was too individualistic, too open to interpretation and enigma. *Odalisque in Red Trousers* worked because it conformed to the classical (read idealized and generalized) tradition of draftsmanship and repeated the now clichéd subject of the Oriental woman. Achieving the zenith of its modern empire after the war, France sought to reshape its national identity, investing yet more of its prestige into the image of a great imperial power.[27] Far from moribund, Orientalism provided a clear and stable tradition which could unite the French, as it had in Delacroix's day, suppressing political differences at home while reasserting the moral and sexual chasm that separated them from their colonized peoples.

Western representations of Oriental women and the discourse of Orientalism were only severely tested with the onset of decolonization following World War II. In December 1954, only six weeks after both the beginning of the Algerian Revolution and the death of Matisse, Picasso began a series of drawings, fifteen paintings and a suite of lithographs based on the theme of Delacroix's *Women of Algiers* (fig. 1). Picasso was well aware that the image of the Oriental woman had become a canonical theme of the grand tradition in Western painting, and that Matisse's death had left him as

the lone heir of that tradition. "When Matisse died," he said, "he left his odalisques to me as a legacy."[28] Yet, when his series was exhibited in 1955, the critic Charles Estienne of *France Observateur* wrote that with Picasso's canvases "one thinks above all, unfortunately, of a vulgar mockery (*chahutage*) of Matisse's odalisques."[29] Something was amiss.

In Algeria itself the status and representation of Algerian women had been contested since the assertion of Arab feminism in the 19th century, and the controversy increased following the outbreak of the Algerian Revolution. Much of the debate concerned the veil. Once a traditional and occasional part of Islam, the veil became a screen for the political projections and goals of all parties. At different times in the Algerian Revolution, wearing or not wearing the veil helped women carry out military missions. Without the veil one might pass in the streets as a Western woman and gain access to important public locales. In other instances, the veil could serve as cover.[30]

A last-ditch effort to control the representation of the Arab woman occurred on May 13, 1958, in a particularly chilling bit of political theater. Immediately following a military coup which ousted French civilian authorities in Algeria,

Figure 4. Henri Matisse, *Odalisque in Red Trousers*, 1921. Oil on canvas, 25½×35½ in. Centre National d'Art et de Culture Georges Pompidou, Paris

Figure 5. Pablo Picasso, *The Women of Algiers, "O,"* 1955. Oil on canvas, 45 x 58 in. Collection Mrs. Victor W. Ganz, New York. Photo courtesy Museum of Modern Art, New York.

the newly governing French military attempted to consolidate the support of its colonials. It assembled Algerian women on the steps in front of the Governor's Palace and stripped them of their veils. Cries of "Vive l'Algérie française!" rang out. Ostensibly, the purpose was to demonstrate France's liberation of Algerian women.[31] Once again, however, the liberationist ideology was used to recall the old saw about Eastern despotism, symbolized by the veil. Algeria's women were really a prop for the new military regime's reassertion of its power over Algerian life. The military's ceremonial unveiling of Algerian women carried out the dictum of the colonial administration as described by Frantz Fanon: "If we want to destroy the structure of Algerian society, its capacity for resistance, we must first of all conquer the women; we must go and find them behind the veil. . . ."[32] In the last years of France's colonial regime, this event repeated and actualized the unveiling of the Oriental woman begun by the presentation of Delacroix's painting in 1834.

In the same years, Picasso's series on the *Women of Algiers* began to take apart this tradition. Although we do not have statements by

Picasso on the outbreak of the Algerian Revolution, we do know that his sympathies lay on the left, with the opponents of an "Algérie française."[33] His extensive series is encyclopedic in its references to Delacroix's and Matisse's works, but it is decidedly conflicted and ambivalent. Picasso does indeed follow the tradition in his presentation of nude and eroticized Oriental women in an interior; the debt to Delacroix is the starting point. Yet, the final picture of the series, *The Women of Algiers, "O"* (fig. 5), for instance, is overtly aggressive and uninviting. Access to the harem is barred by the formidable figure on the left and the otherwise collapsed space which is particularly blocked on the right. Unlike Matisse's *Odalisque in Red Trousers*, the patterning here is not luxuriant and dreamy, but collapsing and jarring, the colors harsh, not warm and sensual. In contrast to the convincingly and alluringly illusionistic torso of Matisse's odalisque, the volumes of Picasso's figures are constricted by harsh, cubistic forms, more like the volumetric passages in the nightmarish visions of Max Beckmann. Only one of Picasso's figures, the one at far left, sits still for the picture, and she is nearly regal and dignified in her posture, gaze and enormous

31. Kamala Ishaq Ibrahim
Loneliness
1987
Oil on canvas
41 x 41 in.
**Collection Jordan National
Gallery of Fine Arts**
Photo courtesy Jordan National
Gallery of Fine Arts

scale. In particular, the figure at lower right refers directly to Matisse's odalisques, especially in her recumbent posture and raised arms. Her legs, however, are neither relaxed nor inviting. Her body, and indeed, the whole interior, is shot through with a violence that is reminiscent of *Guernica*. Whatever Picasso's own psychosexual proclivities and political affiliations, his *Women of Algiers* are either self-possessed or completely given over to other forces. They are unlike Matisse's odalisques and unlike the tradition of the Orientalist's harem women. They are decidedly not complicit.

Since decolonization, Eastern women have continued to be the subject of important cultural, religious and, always, political discussion. The most important change is exemplified by the current exhibition, in which we now hear the voices of Arab women on the subject of their own history. The Algerian novelist and filmmaker Assia Djebar addresses the cultural and political legacy of Western depictions of Oriental women in her 1980 novel named for Delacroix's picture, *Les Femmes d'Alger dans leur appartement*. Djebar sees Delacroix in the role of "the thief, the spy, the voyeur."[34] She perceives the picture as a violation, the women as objects of a keyhole view of the gaze of the artist, and she implies that the image both actively oppresses Oriental women and accurately depicts their oppression. This allows her to discuss the painting's current relevance, for she uses it to warn that Algerian women are "once again with ankles shackled," now under the thumb of a new oppressor.[35] Djebar offers her view of the status of Arab women in the post-colonial era:

"For a few decades—as each nationalism triumphs here and there—we have been able to realize that within this Orient that has been delivered unto itself, the image of woman is still perceived no differently, be it by the father, by the husband, and, more troublesome still, by the brother and the son."[36] In Picasso's *Women of Algiers* she finds an image of freedom that has yet to be attained: "Picasso reverses the malediction, causes misfortune to burst loose, inscribes in audacious lines a totally new happiness. A foreknowledge that should guide us in our everyday life."[37] Whether in reference to Delacroix or Picasso, Djebar's work turns the Western Orientalist tradition on itself and on any other claimants to that patriarchal throne.

The inclusion of work by Houria Niati in the current exhibition confirms that Djebar is not alone in rethinking the Orientalist tradition. An Algerian artist now working in England, Niati grew up during the Algerian Revolution. She was imprisoned for her actions in the revolution, in which she was both participant and witness. Her work, *No to Torture*, 1982–93 (plate 29), brings Delacroix's *Women of Algiers* directly to mind. Niati's "new" women of Algiers are now seen against a darkened background. She will not replicate the luxury and splendor of Delacroix's interior or of his handling of paint. The figures float in darkness, their feet in shackles, their heads in cages. The series is strong and direct. The pictures unmask the power dynamics inherent in Delacroix's picture, while in no way confining their relevance to the oppression of the colonial past.

Finally, the persistence of the Orientalist tradition is confronted by the characters of Leïla Sebbar's 1982 novel, *Shérazade*. This coming-of-age story, set in contemporary Paris, brings together two lovers, the Algerian-born Shérazade and Julien, formerly a French colonial. The two get together despite or, perhaps, because of, their differences. Julien is passionate about 19th-century Orientalist painting, and on their first outing the couple visits the Louvre, where they spend time in front of Delacroix's *Women of Algiers*. Later, Julien explains the conventions of Western images of Oriental women: "They are always stretched out, languishing, their gaze vague, nearly asleep . . . they evoke for the painters of the Occident the nonchalance, the lasciviousness, the perverse seduction of the Oriental woman."[38] By the end of the novel, Shérazade has learned enough.

Although still in love with Julien, she leaves him, and her thoughts turn instantly to her working-class and immigrant friends who would hate paintings in museums, "rotten bourgeois culture, the decadent West, old, played out, dead." While reading in the library of the Beaubourg,[39] she happens by Matisse's *Odalisque in Red Trousers*. At that moment she decides to return to Algeria, but before she departs, she buys a postcard of the painting and writes a farewell: "It's because of her that I'm taking off."[40] This is Shérazade's—and Sebbar's—decisive response to the long legacy of an imperial culture.

Notes

The author would like to extend his thanks to Professor Edward W. Said of Columbia University, and to Professors Robert W. Baldwin and Charlotte Daniels, and Librarians Lorrie A. Knight and Ashley B. Hanson of Connecticut College.

1 Mary Anne Stevens reasserts this traditional view in "Western Art and Its Encounter with the Islamic World, 1798–1914," in *The Orientalists: Delacroix to Matisse: The Allure of North Africa and the Near East* (London: Royal Academy of Arts, 1984), 15–23.

2 Edward W. Said, *Orientalism* (New York: Random, 1978); Linda Nochlin, "The Imaginary Orient," *Art in America* (May 1983): 119–31, 187–191.

3 See, for instance, Alexandre Gabriel Decamps, *Le Musée— Revue du Salon de 1834* (Paris: Abel Ledoux, 1834); and W., "Salon de 1834 (6e article.)," *Le Constitutionel* 101 (11 April 1834): 1.

4 Hilaire-Léon Sazerac, *Lettres sur le Salon de 1834* (Paris: Delaunay, 1834), 143. Unless otherwise indicated, translations from the French are the author's.

5 Philippe Burty, "Eugène Delacroix à Alger," *L'Art* 32, no. 1 (1883): 76.

6 Georges Marçais, *Le Costume Musulman d'Alger* (Paris: Plon, 1930), 121–23.

7 Ernest-Théodore Hamy, *Les Origines du Musée Ethnographique: Histoire et Documents* (Paris: Ernest Leroux, 1890), 38–45, 125–36.

8 Maurice Regard, "Eugène Delacroix et le Comte de Mornay au Maroc (1832), (Documents Inédits)," *Etudes d'art* 7 (1952): 31–33.

9 Elie Lambert, *Delacroix et 'Les Femmes d'Alger'* (Paris: H. Laurens, 1937), 10.

10 Raymond Escholier, *Delacroix et les femmes* (Paris: Fayard, 1963), 81–82.

11 Burty, "Eugène Delacroix à Alger," 96.

12 Escholier, *Delacroix et les femmes*, 81–82.

13 Decamps, *Le Musée—Revue du Salon de 1834*, 57–58.

14 Gabriel Laviron, *Le Salon de 1834* (Paris: Louis Janet, 1834), 88–89. On the West's view of the harem as the ultimate site of Asiatic despotism, see the excellent book by Alain Grosrichard, *Structure du sérail: La Fiction du despotisme Asiatique dans l'Occident classique* (Paris: Seuil, 1979).

15 Gustave Planche, "De l'Ecole Française au Salon de 1834," *Revue des Deux-Mondes* (1 April 1834): 458–61.

16 Antoine-Ignace Melling, *Voyage pittoresque de Constantinople et des rives du Bosphore*, 2 vols. (Paris: P. Didot l'aîné, 1819).

17 Melling, vol. 1, n.p.

18 Melling, vol. 1, 1.

19 Lithograph by Adolphe Richard. An example is in the Bibliothèque Nationale, Paris, Département des Estampes, Qb1 1830 (5 July).

20 Dominique Bernasconi discusses these prints in "L'image de l'Algérie dans l'iconographie française (1830–1871)," (Paris: Mémoire, Institut d'Etudes Politiques de l'Université de Paris, 1970).

21 André Jardin and André-Jean Tudesq, *Restoration and Reaction, 1815–1848*, trans. E. Forster (Cambridge: Cambridge University Press, 1988), 160.

22 One of a series of lithographs by B. Roubaud, *Les Troupiers en Afrique*, 1844–45.

23 Sarah Graham-Brown, *Images of Women: The Portrayal of Women in Photography of the Middle East, 1860–1950* (New York: Columbia University Press, 1988), 39.

24 In *The Colonial Harem*, trans. Myrna Godzich and Wlad Godzich (Minneapolis, Minn.: University of Minnesota Press, 1986), Malek Alloula makes a psychoanalytic argument for the function of colonial postcards and reproduces this one. See p. 115.

25 A point wisely made in relation to recent Matisse exhibitions. See Roger Benjamin, "Matisse in Morocco: A Colonizing Esthetic?" *Art in America* (November 1990): 157–64, 211, 213; also see Linda Nochlin, "'Matisse' and Its Other," *Art in America* (May 1993): 88–97.

26 Kenneth E. Silver, *Esprit de Corps: The Art of the Parisian Avant-Garde and the First World War, 1914–1925* (Princeton, N.J.: Princeton University Press, 1989), 264.

27 Kenneth E. Silver, "Matisse's Retour à l'ordre," *Art in America* (June 1987): 110–123, 167, 169. Regarding the more recent use of Matisse's Orientalism, Roger Benjamin notes how the exhibition *Matisse in Morocco*, sponsored by the United States and the Soviet Union, functioned as "an esthetic token for the resolution of political differences." He observed that the avoidance of the politics of Matisse's Orientalism in the catalogue corresponded to the show's obfuscation of the superpowers' own neocolonial posture vis-à-vis the Islamic world. Benjamin, "Matisse in Morocco," 159, 161.

28 Quoted in Marie-Laure Bernadac, "Picasso 1953–1972: Painting as Model," in *Late Picasso: Paintings, Sculpture, Drawings, Prints 1953–1972* (London: Tate Gallery, 1988), 55.

29 Charles Estienne, "Picasso ou le Dernier Portrait,"
    France Observateur, 16 June 1955, 26. Quoted by Kay Dian
    Kriz, "Picasso's Variations on Delacroix's *Femmes d'Alger*:
    The Grand Tradition, Desire and Colonialism (Again),"
    unpubl. paper, University of British Columbia (1987), 15.
    I am indebted to Professor Kriz for her work on the
    Picasso series.

30 For an overview of Arab feminism, see the introduction to
    Margot Badran and Miriam Cooke, eds., *Opening the Gates:
    A Century of Arab Feminist Writing* (Bloomington, Ind.:
    Indiana University Press, 1990). For a discussion of the
    veil in the Algerian Revolution, turn to Marie-Aimée
    Helie-Lucas, "Women, Nationalism and Religion in the
    Algerian Liberation Struggle," in Badran and Cooke,
    Opening the Gates, 105–114. See also Chapter 8, "The
    Discourse of the Veil," in Leila Ahmed, *Women and Gender
    in Islam: Historical Roots of a Modern Debate* (New Haven,
    Conn.: Yale University Press, 1992).

31 Marnia Lazreg, "Gender and Politics in Algeria:
    Unraveling the Religious Paradigm," *Signs* 15, no. 4
    (Summer 1990): 755–80.

32 Frantz Fanon, *A Dying Colonialism*, trans. H. Chevalier
    (New York: Grove Weidenfeld, 1965), 37–38.

33 Kriz, "Picasso's Variations on Delacroix's *Femmes d'Alger*."
    On the formal development of the series, see the classic
    essay by Leo Steinberg, "The Algerian Women and
    Picasso at Large," in *Other Criteria: Confrontations with
    Twentieth-Century Art* (London: Oxford University Press,
    1972), 125–234.

34 Assia Djebar, *Women of Algiers in Their Apartment*, trans. M.
    de Jager (Charlottesville, Va: University of Virginia Press,
    1992), 137.

35 Djebar, *Women of Algiers*, 2.

36 Djebar, 138.

37 Djebar, 149.

38 Leïla Sebbar, *Shérazade: 17 ans, brune, frisée, les yeux verts*
    (Paris: Stock, 1982), 189–190. Sebbar's mother was
    French and her father Algerian. For a very informative
    article on writers Djebar and Sebbar, see Mildred
    Mortimer, "Language and Space in the Fiction of Assia
    Djebar and Leïla Sebbar," *Research in African Literatures*
    18 (Fall 1988): 301–11.

39 Centre National d'Art et de Culture Georges Pompidou.

40 Sebbar, *Shérazade*, 238, 245, 252.

Modern Arab Art

An Overview

Wijdan Ali

In the 16th century all Arab lands (except Morocco) became part of the Ottoman Empire. By the end of the 19th century the Islamic world in general, and the Arab countries in particular, had reached their lowest ebb politically, economically and culturally. Weak and corrupt rulers, government incapacity, wasteful imperialistic enterprises fostered by the Ottomans and a succession of internal uprisings all led to a widespread feeling of despondency and an increasing reliance upon Western powers—hardly a climate conducive to the development of the arts. The decline of traditional Islamic arts was accompanied by the weakening of political institutions, the corruption of governing bodies and the deterioration of the regional economies of the entire Arab world. These phenomena were interrelated; as the aesthetic and creative fiber of Islamic art declined, it yielded increasingly to Western art forms and styles which had already pervaded the Arab world as a consequence of the West's political, economic, scientific and military hegemony. With the advent of colonialism, the growing communication between East and West exposed the Arab world to a rising tide of European influences.

The development of modern art in the Arab world has been divided into three stages, which apply to almost all Arab countries regardless of the time frame in which they occurred:

The learning stage: The quickest way for Arab artists to "catch up" with Western art trends was to adapt to European traditions and aesthetics. These traditions were passed on to Arab art students by Western instructors at the newly created art schools, as well as by the local aristocracy, who were often strong proponents of Western styles. Inspired by progressive ideas imported from Europe, Arab artists would execute portraits, landscapes and still lifes in the classical manner of the Renaissance and Orientalism. Western political ideologies—starting with the French Revolution and Napoleon's Egyptian expedition—as well as the literary, philosophical and artistic movements originating in Europe during the 19th and early 20th centuries, had the effect of liberating Arab intellectuals, including Islamic artists, from the traditions that had circumscribed them. Such revolutionary movements offered Arab artists a means of realizing their national aspirations based on the doctrines of liberty and equality.

The self-discovery stage: Their training in the Western academic style (which was almost extinct in Europe by the last decades of the 19th century) gave Arab artists a measure of confidence. Yet this newfound assurance made them aware not only of the existing discontinuity between their present and the past, but also between themselves and the general public—between their artistic visions and the state of the world around them. At this second stage, Arab artists endeavored to bridge these disparities by choosing local subjects and themes with which the local public could identify. Thus portraits of peasant women replaced those staple Western images of nymphs and society ladies, and scenes of European-style landscapes gave way to depictions of Lebanese, Egyptian, Iraqi and Syrian countryside.

The search-for-identity stage: After World War II, Western colonialism in the Middle East was in decline. Arabic peoples began a rediscovery of their heritage, taking pride in their nationalism and newfound political independence. It was this cultural reawakening which led to the third stage in the

32. Rabia Sukkarieh
Sheherezade 101
1989
Installation detail
Mixed media panels
15 x 15 in. each
Collection of the artist
Photos by Bruce Wright

development of contemporary art in the Arab world. This search for national identity was preceded by several decades of stylistic homogeneity, during which Western tradition, rather than experimentation, was the guiding principle. Remaining safely in the sphere of the familiar, Arab artists continued to depict local scenes in recognized international styles, such as Impressionism and Postimpressionism. Gradually, however, a growing number of Arab artists began to realize that despite their inculcation into European traditions, they were not, after all, Westerners, no matter how hard they strove to be. With this new realization Arab artists confronted a new dilemma. They felt torn between their present—so visibly and intellectually influenced by the West—and their past, with all its traditions, which represented the only means by which they could safeguard their threatened identity. This cultural paradox induced them to develop an indigenous art language based on traditional elements of Arabic art—including the arabesque, two-dimensional Islamic miniature painting, Arabic calligraphy, Eastern church icons, archaeological figures, ancient and modern legends, folk tales, Arabic literature and social and political events—but employing contemporary media and modes of interpretation.

Like the birth of all art movements, the rise of Arab modernism was an evolutionary process, influenced by factors both cultural and political. The three stages of discovery described here provide a framework in which to study these factors—the "forces of change" affecting the Arab world. Among the countries included in this study are: Egypt, Lebanon, Iraq, Algeria, Tunisia, Morocco, Syria, Jordan, Palestine, Sudan and the states of the Arabian Peninsula. Each is examined in chronological order according to the point at which Western art movements were introduced. We begin with a discussion of Egypt and Lebanon, as it has been established that modern art developed first in these countries.

Egypt

Egypt was the first Arab country to formally embrace Western art. Napoleon's invasion of 1798 took the country completely by surprise, abruptly exposing it to European aesthetics, which Egypt's urban intellectuals quickly absorbed. When the military campaign ended, a number of French scientists and artists stayed on to study and record the monuments and paint native scenes. Many of them adopted local dress and integrated themselves into Arab society. Such efforts at acculturation facilitated the transmission of Western painting into Egypt.

In the aftermath of the French withdrawal, Muḥammad 'Alī Pāshā came to power in 1805 as effective ruler of Egypt. He soon made clear his aspirations of transforming Egypt into a modern country. Not only was he determined that his people should master European science and military technology, he also displayed great interest in the arts, sending several study missions to Europe to learn engraving, painting and sculpture, among other subjects. Upon returning to Egypt, these artists taught at technical craft schools, their instruction of Western techniques replacing traditional methods. Foreign architects and artists created the palaces and public parks built during Muḥammad 'Alī's reign, filling them with artwork of baroque and rococo design. During this time a number of foreign artists visited Egypt, among them the Orientalists David Roberts, Eugène Fromentin, Théodore Frère and William Holman Hunt. Some artists, like John Frederick Lewis and Jean Léon Gérôme, settled in Cairo for months, sometimes years. Thus the inculcation of Western art styles was virtually assured by this steady stream of European influence.

Under the rule of Khedive Ismā'īl (1862–1879), Egypt became virtually independent of the Ottoman Empire, continuing the impetus to establish modern institutions begun by Muḥammad 'Alī. The opening of the Suez Canal in 1869 was an occasion that further accelerated Egypt's exposure to Western culture. Eventually, Western artistic influences pervaded the Egyptian upper classes. In 1891 the Orientalist painters living in Egypt organized the first exhibition ever presented at the Opera House. The Khedive attended to demonstrate his support of the Western art movement, and a number of dignitaries followed his example by purchasing works—though this display of enthusiasm was fueled by their desire to please him rather than pure appreciation.

Spurring on the aesthetic changes precipitated by foreign visitors were influential groups within Egypt itself. From the turn of the century until the 1950s, artists from Egypt's

Greek and Italian communities, situated mainly in Alexandria, were instrumental in promoting Western styles among local artists.

By the beginning of the 20th century members of Egypt's intelligentsia had begun to embrace nationalism. They advocated independence through peaceful means, such as educating and mobilizing masses of people in progressive action programs. One of the members of this group was Prince Yūsuf Kamâl, an enthusiastic patron of the arts who took it upon himself to initiate his people's "education of taste." In 1908 he established the School of Fine Arts in Cairo—the first art institution in the Arab world to offer instruction in Western styles and techniques. Believing local artists to be unqualified, he employed foreign artists as teachers in his new school. To further increase contact with the West, Egypt also began to send its artists abroad for further training. In 1911 Maḥmūd Mukhtār (who would later achieve fame as one of the innovators of the modern art movement) became the first student to receive such a scholarship. Upon graduating from the School of Fine Arts, he was sent by Prince Yūsuf Kamâl to the École des Beaux Arts in Paris. The Egyptian government has been sending artists to train at Western academies on a regular basis since 1917. Following the 1952 Revolution, many of these scholarship recipients entered art institutions in the former Eastern Bloc as well as in the West. Returning home, the graduates became teachers in Egypt's various art colleges and institutes, to ensure the further spread of European ideas.

The students who first attended Cairo's School of Fine Arts—including Maḥmūd Mukhtār, Mohammad Nagy, Maḥmūd Sa'īd, Raghib 'Ayyād, Yūsuf Kāmil and Habīb Gorgī—comprised the nucleus of the pioneer generation of modern Egyptian artists. Incorporating the nationalistic spirit of the time in their work, they represented the struggle of their nation against colonialism by drawing on ancient Eastern traditions in painting and sculpture and linking them to Western art styles. They broke away from the structures of the European academic school, paving the way for a national Egyptian school of art. An important figure in the early development of the modern art movement was Maḥmūd Mukhtār (1891–1934), whose forms would later be referred to as the neopharaonic style. Mukhtār used ancient hieroglyphic symbolism and borrowed a classical structural stylization for the formation of his figures, always imparting a thematic quality to his work. By adapting Western techniques and training to his rich cultural and artistic heritage, Mukhtār presented Egyptian art with a new identity that disseminated nationalistic ideas without resorting to xenophobia.

The members of Egypt's artistic vanguard laid down the basic concepts of their country's modern art movement. They tried to combine their ancient artistic traditions with contemporary techniques and teachings, reshaping them within a distinct Egyptian individuality that emerged out of the country's pharaonic and Mediterranean past. Depicting local subjects, the first graduates of the School of Fine Arts expressed the nationalistic fervor building in their country, basing this sentiment on Egypt's pharaonic legacy.

Unlike other Arab countries, Egypt by the turn of the century could already boast a growing number of women artists, who had began painting even before the School of Fine Arts was established. Included in this group were the sculptor Princess Samīha Ḥusain (daughter of Sulṭān Ḥusain Kāmil), the famous women's rights activist Ḥuda Sha'rāwī, and Nafīsa Aḥmad 'Abdīn. Their work was purely academic with some impressionistic overtones, yet they were the precursors to a definite shift toward modernism. That women's achievements were being recognized at such an early period is a measure of Egypt's accelerated advancement into the modern age.

Since the 1920s the state has played an important role in the development of the modern art movement in Egypt. Appreciating the importance of its own artists, the Ministry of Education started collecting Egyptian works as early as 1925. The Egyptian Parliament simultaneously legislated to guarantee artists freedom of expression and bestow on the arts official protection. One bill recommended special attention for the visual arts and, in 1927, Parliament legislated to approve the establishment of the Museum of Modern Art in Cairo, which opened in 1931.

The Egyptian government also promoted art training for young women. When the Ministry of Education introduced drawing and painting lessons into the curricula, girls' schools were included in the program as well. The art

33. Gazbia Sirry
The Promenade
1993
Oil on canvas
29 1/2 x 39 1/2 in.
Collection of the artist

34. Nazli Madkour
Oasis
1990
Mixed media and
papyrus on canvas
39 1/2 x 39 1/2 in.
Collection of the artist
Photo by Mark Gulezian

teachers and inspectors were all British, and art lessons concentrated on copying and enlarging upon accepted pictures. 'Afīfa Tawfīq was the first female student to be sent on a funded art scholarship to England in 1924. A year later she was joined by Zainab 'Abdu, Iskandara Gabriel and 'Ismat Kamāl. They returned to Egypt after four years to work as art instructors at girls' schools. Following in their footsteps, Alice Tādrus, 'Adālat Ṣidqī, In'ām Sa'īd and Kawkab Yūsuf went to England to study. Upon their return, they introduced modern teaching methods employing psychology in art education. A number of prominent women artists have since come out of Egypt, including Marguerite Nakhle, whose early works demonstrate influences of ancient Coptic art; Tahia Halim, whose stylized figures recall pharaonic wall paintings; Zeinab Abdel Hamid with her linear style; Gazbia Sirry; Inji Efflatoun; and Rabāb Nemr.

The Higher Institute of Fine Arts for Female Teachers was the first art academy for girls, established in 1939 by the government under the directorship of the painter Zainab 'Abdu (b. 1906). In 1947 it became a coeducational Higher Institute for Art Teachers and, in 1970, it was transformed again, becoming the College of Art Education.

When the revolution broke out in 1952, Egyptian artists found themselves living in a new political atmosphere. They lost no time in expressing their newfound freedoms, espousing the slogans of the revolution which supported the same ideals of liberty and equality that some had been trying to promote earlier. A new crop of artists appeared who portrayed Egyptian nationalism through symbolism. They hailed their country's independence from foreign rule and bureaucratic nepotism, welcoming the end of a privileged aristocratic class. They glorified the Egyptian peasant, who had always been featured in modern Egyptian art, along with manual laborers and other segments of the working classes. With growing frequency they depicted popular ceremonies of pilgrimage and marriage, marketplace scenes and folk traditions, such as the celebration of the Prophet Muḥammad's birthday among the poor. These works were met with official and popular appreciation which encouraged artists in their endeavors to extol local character and displace European aesthetics. Despite numerous attempts to

develop indigenous artistic trends, however, strategies for reviving public pride in Egypt's cultural heritage remained vague until 1958. Interestingly enough, while Egyptian artists were attempting to look within to discover a new national perspective based on traditional themes, the art world was beginning to focus on concepts of international art and modernization.

The nationalization of the Suez Canal by Gamal Abdel Nasser, followed by the Tripartite Aggression, intensified patriotic fervor among all Egyptians, including artists. The new trend which developed at this time was based on the philosophy of Pan-Arabism, which was popularized by Nasser's attempts to create Arab unity under his leadership. The idea of combining Egyptian legacy with modernity found substance in the form of a quest for an Arab national artistic identity, completely free of all manner of imported artistic influences. In response to this new cultural trend, one group of artists referred to Egyptian rural life, finding in its customs a connection to religious and folk traditions. In their search for continuity, these artists continued what their predecessors had already begun at the beginning of the 20th century. A second group drew on ancient Egyptian artistic traditions to assert a national artistic identity. Again, the continuity between these artists and those of the previous generation was unmistakable. A third group of artists turned to their Islamic heritage. Their exploration into its aesthetics resulted in the formation of geometric abstraction inspired by ancient arabesque designs and the gestural qualities of classical Arabic calligraphy. A parallel trend to these three was a fourth which fostered internationalism in art and followed known Western styles ranging from Impressionism to Expressionism, Abstraction and Pop Art. These three approaches to contemporary art continue to inspire artists today.

After Egypt's defeat in the 1967 Six-Day War with Israel, its art movement suffered a period of stagnation. Artistic torpor was relieved in 1973, when Anwar Sadat's open-door policy inspired a renewed surge of creativity. The number of exhibition halls increased throughout Egypt, and foreign cultural centers were reactivated. A new National Center for the Arts (including an opera house) opened and the Cairo Biennial was inaugurated in 1982, modeled on its Alexandrian sister.

Lebanon

By the beginning of the 17th century, Emir Fakhr-al-dīn II, a local potentate, ruled the whole of Ottoman Lebanon. In 1613 he visited the Medici Court in Florence and was impressed by the Renaissance art and architecture. Upon his return to Lebanon he decided to open his country to the mainstream of Western civilization by ruling according to contemporary Western methods and launching an open-door policy towards Europe. His rule marked the beginning of a new era for the country, particularly the areas along the Lebanese coast.

Lebanon under Ottoman rule was divided into different administrative districts, among them, Mount Lebanon. This region retained a strong sense of individuality under its feudal and religious system. It was Europe's missionary zeal during the mid-19th century that brought the early currents of Westernization to the mountains of Lebanon. In addition to evangelization, Christian missionaries also sought to propagate Western art forms, introducing the printing press to the region, as well as Western-style painting and, to a lesser extent, sculpture.

The Church was the foundation for all cultural, social and political life, and this new religion stimulated the emergence of an intellectual and artistic awakening. In accordance with ecclesiastical tastes, Gothic style became popular in 18th-century Lebanon and eventually gave birth to a local Gothic school of religious painting. Icons, portraits of patriarchs and simple religious scenes with a hierarchic flavor filled the numerous churches and convents in mountain towns and villages. Thus, while the arts flourished in Lebanon, they were bound to the aesthetics of the Church and followed an established pattern of European design.

By the 18th century, however, secular art imported from Italy and Austria began to influence the local talent. Orientalists including David Roberts, William Bartlett, Horace Vernet, Sir David Wilkie, Edward Lear, Carl Haag and Amadeo Preziosi came in droves to Beirut and the Lebanese coast, where they recorded landscapes, ruins and monuments in minute detail.

During the second half of the 19th century, as foreign artists continued to flock to Lebanon, a growing number of Lebanese youths traveled to Istanbul to pursue their studies. As subjects of the Ottoman Empire, some of them matriculated in the Turkish military and naval academies. These art students adhered to trends prevalent among Turkish soldier/artists, which in turn influenced the Lebanese Marine School of painting. Works from the Marine School were characterized by their depictions of the Lebanese coast and often featured luminous beach scenes, historical imagery and handsome ships. While most of these late 19th-century works have, unfortunately, been lost, extant paintings indicate that most of the Lebanese artists of this period were amateurs, lacking academic training and technical skill.

The end of the 19th century ushered in an important era for Lebanese culture. Beirut was already an established bridge between East and West and had acquired a number of Western-style institutions and enterprises, such as a theater, a public library, commercial printing and local newspapers—including an art journal. In addition, the establishment of universities brought an influx of Western influences to the cultural and artistic life of the city.

The early pioneers of Lebanese modern art worked at the end of the 19th and the beginning of the 20th centuries. Most of them traveled to European cities like Brussels, Rome, London and Paris to further their education and to gain firsthand knowledge of classical and contemporary Western practices by visiting museums and the studios of individual artists. Daoud Corm (1852–1930) is a prominent member of this generation of artists. In 1870 he went to Rome and enrolled at the Institute of Fine Arts, where he trained under Roberto Bompiani, the official Italian court painter to Victor Emmanuel II. During his five years in Rome, Corm studied the works of Renaissance artists and was influenced by Raphael, Michelangelo and Titian, whose styles he assimilated in his paintings. He gained official recognition when he was commissioned to paint the portrait of Pope Pius IX, later becoming one of the official painters attached to the Belgian Court of Leopold II. Upon his return to Lebanon, he was much in demand as a portrait painter and was sought out by many distinguished personalities in the Levant and Egypt. These portraits remain a treasure trove of information about the national costumes worn at the end of the 19th and the beginning of the 20th century.

35. Huguette Caland
Foule
1970
Silk
Collection of the artist
Photo by Bruce Wright

36. Huguette Caland
Tendresse
1975
Silk
Collection of the artist
Photo by Bruce Wright

37. Huguette Caland
Tête à Tête
1971
Silk
Collection of the artist
Photo by Bruce Wright

Achieving international acclaim as a painter of religious themes, Corm produced a wealth of art for churches in Lebanon, Syria, Egypt and Palestine. His religious works point to delicate feelings and a deep faith, after the manner of Leonardo da Vinci and the Italian Renaissance painters. They illustrate his view of the human body, which he considered the essence of beauty, devoid of sensuality and voluptuousness.

Corm's influence freed Lebanese art of its previously narrow, amateurish tradition, leading it to the wide perspectives of the great classical masters and thus marking an important step in the history of modern art in Lebanon. He was responsible for training a number of aspiring young artists, including Habib Srūr and Khalil Ṣalībī, whose work, in turn, inspired the next wave of modern artists.

The turn of the century saw a second and quite different generation of modern artists come to the fore in Lebanon. Though they took advantage of the preceding generation's experience and Western training, they turned away from the local genre of religious art. Yūsuf Hoyeck (1883–1962) spent twenty years learning drawing and sculpture in Rome and Paris, where he trained under Henri Bourdelle. He was influenced by Renaissance sculpture and by Auguste Rodin's tormented figures. In 1932 he returned to Beirut and devoted himself to sculpting and teaching. Hoyeck, who is considered the father of modern sculpture in Lebanon, was instrumental in training most artists of the following two generations.

As World War I came to an end in 1918, so too did Ottoman rule over Lebanon. In 1919 the French Mandate was established, and in 1924 mandate authorities made French and Arabic the official languages of Lebanon. It was during this period that a most important generation of Lebanese artists appeared. Its leaders included Muṣṭafa Farrūk (1901–1957), César Gemayel (1898–1958), ʿUmar Onsi (1901–1969), Salībā Dūwaiḥy (b. 1915) and Rāshid Wahbī (b. 1917). They laid the foundation for modern art in Lebanon, and their impact continues to the present day. Their art manifested a spirit of freedom and originality, both in style and media, which had been lacking in the works of the two previous generations. Yet, much credit for this advancement also belongs to their teachers—Corm, Srūr and Ṣalībī—who helped them to gain self-confidence and establish their artistic roots within the intimate atmosphere of their own national culture.

Unlike their predecessors who had been educated in the West, Farrūk, Gemayel, Onsi, Dūwaiḫy and Wahbī received their initial training in Lebanon, only later traveling to Rome and Paris. Upon their return they became instrumental in awakening feelings of national pride in the recent history of their country through their depictions of Lebanon's natural beauty. Their landscape paintings of the mountains and coastline also documented Lebanese art and culture, since they included detailed depictions of architecture and of the people of Lebanon posing in their national dress and practicing local customs. Their realistic style thus served to glorify everyday life. Of the five artists, only Dūwaiḫy would later go on to explore abstraction.

Coming from modest economic backgrounds, these pioneers of modernism rankled at the notion that art was a luxury reserved for the wealthy and powerful. As teachers they were able to pass on to their students the training they had received in the studios of their predecessors, along with the new Western techniques they had learned in European academies. Their talent and dedication were instrumental in introducing Lebanese modernism to the general public, making art accessible to a wider audience.

By the 1930s Beirut was fast becoming a cultural and artistic hub for artists from Lebanon, France and many other countries. Under the auspices of the French Mandate authorities, a series of exhibitions was held to stress the cultural aspects of French policy. Regardless of the ulterior motives, these exhibitions created a stimulating atmosphere which established Beirut's reputation as a center for Arabic, Francophile art. In 1937 Alexis Boutros founded the Académie Libanaise des Beaux Arts in Beirut, further bolstering the city's cultural standing. In addition to French and Italian instructors, he also employed Lebanese teachers, including César Gemayel. With the opening of the Académie, it now became possible for students to a receive professional art education in Lebanon, although many still preferred to go abroad for their training.

After World War II the United States emerged as a popular superpower with ideas of equality and democracy attractive to Arab youths. American culture now began to dominate those art circles where French culture had once held sway. In 1954 the American University of Beirut opened its Department of Fine Arts, employing two American artists as instructors. The most innovative contribution of this department was its art seminars—a series of public lectures and demonstrations that was open to the public and required no artistic prerequisites. This new department and its progressive approach to art education disproved the myth that France alone had a monopoly on culture, thus exposing students to expanded perspectives. Although formal art training began relatively late in Lebanon, by the 1960s several arts institutions in Beirut were providing Lebanese students with a high level of artistic training.

In the 1960s Beirut was firmly entrenched as the cultural center of the Arab world. Artists from other Arab countries flocked to the Lebanese capital, either to expand their training, exhibit their works or immerse themselves in the intellectual atmosphere of a city which offered Western undercurrents and freedom of expression (qualities that were usually lacking in their homelands). Lebanese artists felt free to express their individuality through their work regardless of popular taste. They delved into Lebanon's past for inspiration, spurred on by a desire to confirm their artistic identity. Yet the works that they produced were free of imitation or repetition, generating acclaim both in Lebanon and abroad. These works were characterized by three elements: solid technique; inspiration drawn from rich, indigenous cultural sources, including classical and Islamic components; and artistic experimentation. The activities forming part of the lively cultural scene of the day consisted of exhibitions, lectures, seminars and book signings. Quite a number of commercial galleries prospered. In addition to arts commentaries found in the daily, weekly and monthly periodicals available in Arabic, English and French, critics voiced their opinions through arts publications, which were instrumental in educating their readership in the new trends. A sophisticated public showed considerable enthusiasm for collecting artwork, which led to a boom in the market and encouraged artists to increase their output while maintaining high standards. Thus a dynamic relationship developed between artists, critics, art dealers and the public.

38. Amal Ftouni
Pattern & Women
1990
Computer generated
photograph, pixel paint
8 x 10 in.
Collection of the artist

39. Nada Raad
Masque
1990
Bronze
15³/4 x 13 x 6 in.
Base: 29 x 14 x 7 in.
Collection Jan M. Lilac

40. Oumaya Alieh Soubra
Espace Lumière
1992
Oil on Japanese paper
23 1/2 x 35 1/2 in.
Collection of the artist

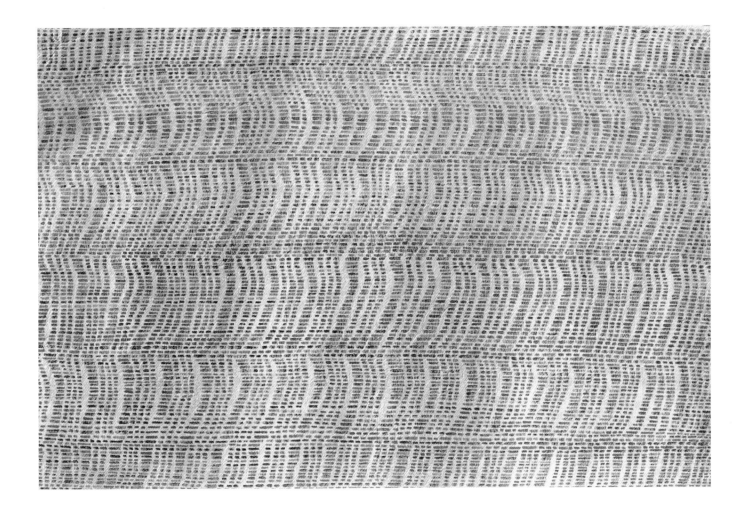

41. Ida Alamuddin
Overflow
1993
Collage, charcoal and oil
29 x 22 in.
Collection of the artist

It flourished in an atmosphere of complete intellectual freedom devoid of interference either from the state or from pressure groups.

The modern art movement in Lebanon eventually interacted with other international movements, inspiring seasoned artists to bold experimentation. This can be seen, for instance, in the work of Etel Adnan (b. 1925), poet, literary critic and painter. After studying literature at the Sorbonne and Harvard universities and establishing herself as a writer, Adnan discovered she possessed a strong inclination toward visual expression. She experimented with different media, but the poet in her was always present in her calligraphic paintings, ceramics and tapestries. In fact, most of her works are actually abstract illustrations of poems. She scribbles verses on painted backgrounds creating accordion-like folios reminiscent of oriental manuscripts. For Adnan, painting is a language without limit which gives her the freedom to express herself both verbally and graphically.

The Lebanese civil war, which broke out in 1975, dealt a severe blow to one of the most flourishing modern art movements in the Arab world. It disrupted all social, political and moral order, bringing the development of the arts to a complete standstill. The qualities of sophistication and innovation which had taken artists decades to achieve were destroyed overnight, leaving behind an aftermath of despair and a sense of banality. The humiliation of the Israeli invasion of South Lebanon in 1978 and that of Beirut in 1982, the breakdown of the economic order and the sectarian and political strife, which was both bloody and senseless, created nearly impossible living conditions throughout the country. The prevalent state of lawlessness gave rise to terrorism and domination by a militia whose creed was "might is right"—only the fittest were able to survive.

Art patronage by the state, the affluent middle class and the intelligentsia ceased, causing cultural and artistic activity to suffer. Foreign cultural centers and commercial galleries closed down. Universities held classes sporadically, depending on the extent of the fighting and violence. A considerable number of talented, recognized artists left the country to live abroad, mostly in Europe and the United States. Those who remained behind had to make the difficult choice between upholding their artistic standards and starving or succumbing to the prevalent vulgar taste to survive.

Such conditions precipitated the rise of two very different trends on the Lebanese art scene. Artists following the first and most common fashion produced saleable, decorative works that copied Islamic motifs and the realism practiced by earlier generations of Lebanese artists. These bland, folkloric paintings, lacking any personal interpretation or innovation, almost replaced the expressiveness and individuality of style that had predominated in earlier decades. The second trend was fostered by artists who stayed in Beirut and continued to paint in isolation from the general public. Some drew on calligraphy and other traditional forms, presenting them from a novel perspective and original aesthetic which added a modern dimension to their heritage. This is the case with Etel Adnan's work. A number of artists had to travel to other capitals inside and outside the Arab world to exhibit their work. Despite the commitment of these innovators, however, Lebanon's art movement suffered a major setback. Yet judgement against those artists who produced for market tastes should be withheld. The cruel living conditions artists suffered during the longest period of internal strife their country had ever experienced certainly contributed to a state of creative impotence. The civil war lasted for sixteen years, coming to an end in 1991. In the brief period since peace has come, cultural and artistic life already has started to revive in Lebanon.

Iraq

Easel painting in oils was introduced to Iraq at the turn of the century by a group of officers who had received art training at military schools in Istanbul. Although they sought to share their knowledge of Western painting techniques by teaching at secondary schools and offering private lessons, their influence was limited to members of the educated upper class, who were among the few supporters of the visual arts in Iraq at this time. Nevertheless, the work of the artists educated by the soldier-painters became the catalyst for the development of modern art in Iraq. The most important figure in this group was Abdul Qadir al-Rassam (1882–1952). Al-Rassam had trained at the Turkish Military Academy and painted in the same naive manner as the Turkish soldier-painters, executing numerous canvases of landscapes and military scenes in a cold, academic manner with little regard for perspective.

Iraq was under British mandate from the end of World War I until 1932, and during this period several reforms were introduced. The British opened eight secondary schools in the capital in 1919. By 1920 there were twenty daily papers and six periodicals being published in Baghdad. As a renewed cultural and political consciousness began to stir among the people, literature and music witnessed a revival and traditional crafts thrived, although innovations in painting were slow to develop.

In the 1920s and 1930s a small group of painters emerged who considered themselves art teachers rather than artists. Their efforts were encouraged by the state, which increased its support of cultural activities and arts education during the 1930s. In 1931, at the behest of Faisal I, the Iraqi government began allocating scholarship funds for art studies abroad. At the same time the state also was conscious of the need for better educational facilities at home. In 1936 the Ministry of Education founded the Music Institute in Baghdad. So successful was the school that it was soon expanded to included departments of drama, painting and sculpture. By 1940–41 the Institute of Music became the Institute of Fine Arts.

Remarkably, no instructors from outside of Iraq taught at the institute. The Iraqi artists initially trained their students in drawing, painting and sculpture according to their own acquired knowledge of Western concepts of art and aesthetics. This preference for Western art resulted from a desire among Iraqi intellectuals to become acquainted with all aspects of European thought and culture, a tendency which grew with the outbreak of World War II. The public responded favorably to new ideas because of the increasing contact with Western countries, especially England, which had the strongest presence in Iraq. These ideas appeared advanced and unusual in comparison to the Ottoman ideologies upon which they were raised. By the 1940s the fine arts had already become part of intellectual life in Iraq, and in 1941 the first art society was formed. That same year the Society of the Friends of Art—founded by artists, architects and art aficionados—presented its first group show for both professionals and amateurs.

The war years also served to stimulate interest in the arts by increasing contact with Eastern Europe. During World War II a group of Polish officers came to Baghdad with the Allied troops. Among them were several artists, two of whom had studied painting with Pierre Bonnard. They introduced Iraqi artists to the latest European styles and advanced the concept that painting should incorporate a personal viewpoint and should not consist merely of copying the sublime forms of nature. These Polish artists played a significant role in acquainting Iraqi painters with trends in modern art that had originated in Europe (including Impressionism, Cubism and expressionism). The Poles were responsible for causing artists to break their ties with the cold academic style popular in Iraq at the time. Their influence was the latest in a chain of events affecting the development of modern art in Iraq. It was this combination of factors—the opening of the Institute of Fine Arts, the provision of art scholarships for study abroad, the involvement of the Polish artists with their local counterparts and the activities of the Society of the Friends of Art—which helped to shift Iraq's modern art movement from its limited boundaries into a broader, international scope of reference.

The most important figure in the modern art movement was Jawād Salim (1919–1961), who guided Iraq toward internationalism. Salim studied in Paris, Rome and London, going on to became head of the Department of Sculpture at the Institute of Fine Arts in Baghdad. He encouraged his students to draw on their cultural heritage of Babylonian and Islamic art traditions to create a distinctive Iraqi art. Salim was probably the first Arab artist to embark on a quest for a national artistic identity within modern concepts. Unlike the pioneers of the Egyptian and Lebanese modern art movements, who depicted their people and landscapes in a realistic manner, Salim used folk motifs as symbols to denote an Iraqi artistic identity. He believed it was the artist's duty to interpret the sentiments of his society by chronicling his country's current events. Thus he became the mirror of Iraq's social conditions. Salim was a painter and sculptor who executed his most mature paintings in the 1950s, establishing an Iraqi style that drew heavily on formal and folk traditions. His style awakened a latent sense of nationalism and induced many Iraqi artists to emulate him.

On June 14, 1958, a bloody revolution led by a group of military officers toppled Iraq's constitutional monarchy. This brought to an end a

42. Helen Khal
Horizon of Peace
1986
Oil on canvas
39 1/2 x 49 1/4 in.
Collection of the artist

period of intense cultural growth during which the visual arts, literature and music flourished alongside social, educational and economic advances. Prior to the 1958 revolution, artists in all fields participated in a thriving market, enjoying public and private patronage. The military coup was a jolt that shook the burgeoning art movement. Artists were torn between succumbing to the new dictatorship's taste for propaganda images or safeguarding their freedom of expression and risking obscurity and recrimination. A few of those who chose the latter course had to leave the country. The rest resigned themselves to the new regime in the hopes that political conditions would improve.

The unsettled political situation in Iraq during the early 1960s, marked by numerous coups d'état, military dictatorships, state censorship, local uprisings and mass executions, created an unhealthy atmosphere that arrested cultural development. The appointments of deans and professors at Baghdad University and the Academy of Fine Arts were dictated by political affiliations rather than academic or artistic qualifications. Most of the artists employed by the government were communists. The untimely death of Jawād Salim in 1961 at the age of forty-one mired the art movement in further stagnation. By the mid-1960s, however, young artists began to return to Iraq after completing their studies in Western Europe, the United States, the former Soviet Union, Poland and China. Some of these newcomers managed to inject the foundering art movement with new blood. Salim's spirit had imbued many Iraqi modern artists with an abiding sense of discipline and a longing to break through domestic boundaries into the Arab world and toward internationalism. Modern communications simultaneously moved beyond local styles and paved the way for further international art exchanges. In 1962 the National Museum of Modern Art was inaugurated. A project which had been conceived during the monarchy, it was funded by the Calouste Gulbenkian Foundation and housed a collection of contemporary Iraqi art.

After the 1958 revolution cultural affairs were administered by the Ministry of National Guidance (the Ministry of Information), which allocated a considerable budget for the arts. After the revolution of 1968 it began to acquire works of art from almost all practicing Iraqi artists. The Ministry also began to pre-sent international and local art exhibitions, as well as literary festivals and seminars.

The 1968 revolution ushered in a new open-door policy. Subsequently, several exhibitions of Iraqi art were presented in other Arab cities, including Cairo, Damascus, Rabat and Beirut. As official state patronage increased, the National Museum of Modern Art multiplied its acquisitions of local artworks and started participating in international biennials and exhibitions. Group exhibitions became more frequent, especially those offered in conjunction with national festivities and important political events. Thus, for several decades, Iraqi artists have benefitted from their government's support, which helped them to revive an active modern art movement in their country.

Algeria

In 1830 Algeria was under French occupation, and by 1847 it had become part of the French republic. Casting itself in the role of "civilizing" conqueror, France vigorously set about the task of assimilating its new citizenry into the Western fold. A concerted effort was made to force Algerians to assume a French identity. The official language became French, education followed the same curricula as in France and the teaching of Arabic was limited to religious schools, where only the Qur'ān was taught. Students read French and European history instead of their own, and Algerians actually were considered French citizens, subject to French law. When the country gained its independence in 1962, the majority of Algerians no longer spoke Arabic—their mother tongue had become French after 159 years of colonization.

In 1832 Eugène Delacroix became the first French painter to visit the newly acquired territory of Algeria. A considerable number of French Orientalists followed in his footsteps. In Algiers they discovered an exotic world which inspired their art, so much so that some even emigrated to live and work in the new province. Employing descriptive, classical figuration, these artists portrayed their vision of life in Algeria, its local customs and scenery in romantic genre scenes. Chief among their stereotypical themes were depictions of blind beggars, Arab horsemen, reclining nudes in harems and Bedouin encampments. It was the Orientalists who introduced European easel painting to the country. As their number grew,

43. Wijdan
Women of Carbala
1993
Mixed media on
handmade paper
Triptych
53 x 84 1/2 in.
Collection of the artist
Photo courtesy Jordan National
Gallery of Fine Arts

they developed new forums to showcase their work, increasing the influence and prestige of Western-style art. It is significant that the Société des Beaux Arts of Algeria, founded in 1851, restricted its membership to artists of French origin. So popular had the Orientalists become that by 1900 a new museum was founded—the Musée d'Alger—to display the latest of their works.

Yet, despite the overwhelming influence of French Orientalism with its preconceptions and stereotypical views, an Algerian perspective in painting was beginning to emerge. By 1894 the French Orientalist painters of Algeria were numerous enough to organize an annual salon in Paris. In 1897 the Société des Peintres Algériens et Orientalistes was founded in Algiers. There was even an École d'Alger which focused on Algerian subjects with a sensitivity previously lacking in Orientalist works. In 1907 the French Governor, M. Jonnart, founded the Villa 'Abd al-Latīf (Maison des artistes) in Algiers for French artists seeking an environment of complete artistic freedom in North Africa. Similar ateliers were created in other cities. Through the years, ninety artists came to stay in the Villa to practice painting, sculpture and etching. The most important Orientalist artist to influence the development of Western-style art in Algeria was Alphonse-Étienne Dinet (1861–1929), who introduced Western academic teaching to Algeria. Yet, while French painters visited Algeria more than any other North African country, their influence was far stronger on resident, non-Arab artists than on native Algerian artists.

Subsequently, Western art in Algeria was most often produced by the descendants of French settlers, whose works were regarded as superior to those of Algerian artists. In 1920 the French authorities established the École des Beaux Arts in Algiers and staffed it with French teachers who prepared the students to continue their studies at the École des Beaux Arts in Paris. The government established similar schools of fine arts in Oran and Constantine.

French predominance notwithstanding, the Algerian art community was beginning to assert itself, albeit gradually and along Orientalist lines. The first group of native Algerian painters rose to prominence between 1914 and 1928, among them, Azouaou

Mammeri (b. 1886) and 'Abd al-Halīm Hemche (b. 1906). They were followed by Binslimān, Farrakh and Būkarsh. All were known for their neoclassical style, which they displayed in Algerian landscapes and genre scenes executed in the manner of the Orientalists.

At the turn of the century a new trend emerged among native Algerian artists who had maintained their focus on traditional Islamic art, rejecting imported Western painting styles which they regarded as colonialist. Muḥammad Rācim (1896–1974) initiated the trend by developing a style that combined Western three-dimensional perspective, Islamic figuration and Arabic calligraphy. Calligraphy and the art of miniature painting were not just forms of decoration to these painters but also a means of asserting their artistic and national identity. Reaching back to Arabic artistic traditions, Rācim and his followers triggered a movement to counter the widespread Orientalism in French-Algerian painting.

By the end of the 1930s Orientalist and neoclassical themes were exhausted, having deteriorated into debilitated forms of folk art. The evolution of Western-style art in Algeria differed from its development in other Arab countries because it had been imposed, rather than introduced. Moreover, the Algerian art world was also monopolized by the French settlers until the 1950s. Because of the reactionary and conservative attitude of the established artists and art schools in the country, modern Postimpressionist styles only penetrated Algeria in the 1950s. Most trained artists of the 1930s and 1940s either perpetuated the Orientalist and neoclassical styles of the French or developed a naive style akin to their self-taught counterparts.

In 1947 a fifteen-year-old, illiterate orphan named Baya Mahieddine (b. 1931) was lauded by the French critic André Breton as a child prodigy. A self-taught artist, she had begun painting and working with clay in 1943. Baya's style, based on childhood dreams and imagination, incorporated naive, surrealistic forms. Although she constantly used the same figures, she had no rational explanation for them. Born into a poor family and orphaned at the age of five, Baya channeled her grief into a fantasy world of vivid colors—depicting flowers, birds and animals floating against plain backgrounds, defying gravity. Her sincerity of expression captured the attention of France's established artists. When her works were on exhibit at Galerie Adrien Maeght in Paris, Pablo Picasso invited her to his country home in Vallauris and observed her as she kneaded clay into animal forms. Baya's rise to fame in France did not affect her artistic vision, however. As she matured she continued to work in her original surrealistic, naive style.

The majority of Algerian artists who came into their own during the 1950s and 1960s were self-taught. They made a complete break from the old traditions in painting and, by doing so, initiated a modern art movement. Through their travels to France they came into contact with the latest trends in Western painting, but their work differed markedly from that of the French artists. Having suffered deculturation through colonialism, they wanted their work to express their Algerian identity. Two distinct styles emerged. One group of artists proclaimed their nationalism by using such local signs and motifs as Arabic calligraphic symbols and Berber designs in abstract formations; the other depicted the social problems of their country in a personalized, expressionistic style. The most prominent artist among the latter group was Muḥammad Issiakhim (1928–1986).

During the years of resistance against the French, a number of artists fought with the National Liberation Army. Their work at this time decried the horrors of war through scenes of soldiers in trenches. These soldier-artists became extremely popular in Algeria. Their nationalistic works, depicting the War of Independence, were later shown in Tunis, Hanoi, Prague, Shanghai, Warsaw, Peking, Havana and Madrid.

After independence, most Algerian artists living abroad returned to their country to contribute to the development of its modern art movement. The majority of the new generation of artists emerging received their training at Algerian art schools, while fewer were educated abroad. Because they were able to acquire a formal art education at home, these artists' ties with their culture were more established than those of their predecessors, and soon their Arab-Islamic identity reasserted itself. In general, the works of post-independence artists of the 1970s and 1980s are abstract and Abstract Expressionist in style.

They either depict local subject matter through the manipulation of Arab and Berber signs used in local handicraft decorations or ignore traditional elements in favor of international art concepts.

Algeria's modern art development, unlike that of some other Arab nations, has always incorporated a traditional art form—Islamic miniature painting. This medium, together with European Orientalist painting, constituted the basis of contemporary art in Algeria. Such dualism has persisted until the present, so that artists in Algeria continue to either explore their heritage or turn to international styles.

Tunisia

In 1881 Tunisia ceased to be part of the Ottoman Empire, becoming a French Protectorate until its independence in 1955. Even before its dominance by France, however, Tunisia had held great attraction for foreign artists. The early Orientalists often chose historical events pertaining to North Africa's Roman period as the predominant subjects of their paintings. The more stereotypical Orientalist themes—picturesque landscapes, exotic natives, Bedouins, blind men and women, slaves, execution and bath scenes—developed much later, around the turn of the century. They were made popular by a generation of colonial artists who displayed their visions of Tunisia in the Parisian salons, impressing critics and the public with their romantic images of the East.

After their occupation of Tunisia, the French authorities founded the Institut de Carthage in 1894, which became the most important scientific and cultural institution in the colony. Its function was to assert France's cultural and educational superiority and thus legitimize its political and economic control. In the same year the Institut de Carthage organized the first Salon Tunisien in Tunis, marking the formal introduction of Western art into the country. Throughout the first two decades of this century, the salon embraced the Orientalist school of art. The general trend it followed was one of narrow, provincial academic traditions, borne of the conservative French colonial mentality that ran counter to modern currents in Paris.

Founded in 1923, the Centre d'Art was the first art school to open in Tunisia. By 1930 it had became the École des Beaux Arts.

Organized along the lines of similar French institutions, the curriculum consisted of applied courses in drawing, painting, sculpture, decoration and etching, as well as academic courses in perspective and the history of art. The teaching environment was strictly conservative and followed traditional academic methods. Although it was open to all nationalities, the Centre d'Art students, whose ages ranged from sixteen to thirty, were almost exclusively European. In fact, until independence in 1955, the number of Tunisian pupils was negligible in comparison to foreign students.

The numerous foreign colonial artists who lived in Tunisia at the time collectively influenced the development of local talent by introducing Western art to the country. The majority of Tunisian-born, French artists were trained at the École des Beaux Arts and the ateliers organized by the previous generation. After independence they left Tunisia for Europe, but not before leaving their mark on the country's modern art movement. Through teaching at the École des Beaux Arts and participating in the Salon Tunisien, they helped to introduce new Western styles, including Impressionism and Cubism. Identified as the vanguard of Tunisia's modern art scene, they collectively displayed their work in Europe and North Africa, mainly at the Exposition de l'Afrique Française. Consequently, modern Tunisian art developed either on the periphery or within the framework of the annual exhibitions organized by the French.

The second quarter of the 20th century was a period of national struggle for independence in Tunisia. At this time many resident European artists died, leaving the responsibility of developing the modern art movement in Tunisian hands. The most important innovator to influence the formation of modern art in Tunisia was Yaḥyā Turkī (1901–1968), a civil servant and self-taught painter. Turkī exhibited at the Salon d'Automne of 1922. The following year he resigned from his government position to accept a scholarship at the École des Beaux Arts in Tunis. He attended art classes for a few months only, however, preferring the freedom of spontaneously treating the subjects which surrounded him to the restrictions of an academic setting. His choice of subject was a difficult one to pursue, because Tunisian artists were not accorded the same respect as their foreign counterparts. Turkī

nevertheless persevered and created a framework from which to operate in the Tunisian environment, which led to a deeper correlation between his works and the Tunisian way of life. With direct, cheerful colors and minimum detail, he portrayed the old city of Tunis with its inhabitants going about their everyday lives. Turkī broke away from Orientalist stereotypes and expressed the emotions of simple people in a free, sometimes blunt, manner. His style created a new dimension for local painting, inspiring other native artists to imbue their work with an indigenous quality. Because of his great influence, Turkī is considered the father of Tunisian painting. His disciples became the vanguard which formed Tunisia's modern art movement.

Early Tunisian artists were conscious of the rift separating them from their foreign peers living in the country. They felt that genre paintings of domes, picturesque living quarters and other impersonal stereotypes were insufficient to represent their nation and people. Taking a more humanistic approach, they attempted to communicate a sympathetic, realistic view of North Africa by depicting the positive side of family life and social traditions. Thus they broke away from the clichés and exaggerations of the École des Beaux Arts, endeavoring to infuse deeper meaning into their work. This new direction, initiated by Yaḥyā Turkī, continued in the work of 'Ammār Farḥāt.

The first art group in Tunisia to include native artists was the Tunis School, established at the end of the 1940s. Although this group had neither a manifesto nor a list of well-defined and common aims, the members all strove to present their own interpretation of the country through their works. This interpretation was characterized by an adherence to the aesthetic and sentimental values related to their country's traditional way of life and a respect for the validity of its artistic heritage. Diverging from contemporary European styles, they tried to revive traditional art forms, including two-dimensional Islamic miniature painting, Arabic calligraphy, the popular tradition of painting on glass and the techniques of local handicrafts. While the artists of the Tunis school all agreed on a number of aesthetic principles and pursued a specific discipline, each developed his or her own personal style independently. The only common denominator among them was their choice of subject

44. Sabiha Khemir
Shipwreck 2
1993
Ink on paper
8 1/2 x 12 in.
Collection of the artist

matter, which drew on their national heritage. The Tunis School was comprised of pioneers such as Yaḥyā Turkī and ʿAmmār Farḥāt, as well as members of the second generation of artists like Jallāl Ibn ʿAbd Allah (b. 1921), Safiyyah Farḥāt (b. 1924) and Hādī Turkī (b. 1922). Artists of the third post-independence generation also were involved. The Tunis School played an important role in introducing and developing Tunisian modern art. Immediately after independence and continuing until the early 1960s, its philosophy became synonymous with the national, spiritual and material values that many artists believed their work should express.

In the early 1960s a movement began which attempted to lend local character to abstraction by identifying it with traditional culture. Adherents of this trend drew on Arabic calligraphy, elements of arabesque decoration and architectural forms. They explored the correlation between the use of two-dimensional space in Islamic art and modern European expressionism and abstractionism. Abstractionism was the first major movement to oppose the realism of the Tunis School. Soon other competing trends developed to challenge it. Neofigurative painters rejected both abstractionism's disregard for realism and other artists' superficial attempts at classical figuration. Embracing elements of expressionism, Surrealism, neorealism and primitivism, Tunisian artists tore reality apart and reconstructed it according to their personal vision. While contemporary Western trends continued to influence Tunisia's modern art development, various forms of traditional Islamic crafts persisted. This duality inspired artists to infuse Western styles with local features.

Morocco

Modern art in Morocco derived from three major sources: Islamic art, the European Orientalist school of painting (introduced after 1912) and Berber handicrafts. As we have seen, European expansion in the 19th century sparked a growing interest in North African culture, and numerous Orientalist painters came to Morocco. For most Western artists, Morocco meant Tangier, a partly Jewish city that had once been under Portuguese rule and English influence (due to its proximity to Gibraltar). The rest of the country was inaccessible to foreigners, mainly because of the dangers of tribal warfare which made traveling unsafe. Because Morocco had never been

under Turkish rule, it developed an individual character and grandiose architecture which never failed to impress foreign visitors. In addition to Delacroix, the most famous of the Orientalists to visit Morocco, several French, Italian, Swiss and American artists also were drawn to the country. The introduction of easel painting can be dated to the period around 1912, when Morocco became a French Protectorate and a Spanish zone was established on its north Mediterranean coast. Tangier and its environs were under multinational control, administered by France and Spain. After 1912 several European painters came to live in Morocco and formed the "colonial school." Some were officials in the civil service, while others were professionals, such as doctors and lawyers, whose hobby was painting. They became the elite of the European colony, organizing exhibitions and salons and founding artistic societies.

Around 1918 the colonial administration transformed Moroccan historical monuments into ethnographic museums, which included areas devoted to art studios and exhibition halls. These institutions stimulated the formation of artistic associations. During the 1940s local, self-taught artists came into direct contact with resident colonial painters and began to imitate their Orientalist style, albeit in an untrained, primitive manner.

It was during the administrations of Morocco's first French Resident-General, Louis Hubert Gonsalve Lyautey (1912–1916 and 1917–1926), that a particular appreciation for traditional Moroccan culture emerged. He preserved many Islamic monuments and built new administrative buildings and cities, such as Casablanca, that were in harmony with the existing landscape around them. His policy of sustaining indigenous crafts was contrary to the systematic destruction of traditional culture that took place in Algeria. Later Morocco's Director-General of Fine Arts organized and directed the production of crafts and continued Lyautey's nurturing policy. He also played an active role in safeguarding the visual heritage of Morocco through the creation of an archive of popular artistic traditions. Such enlightened policies, which contradicted prevailing European sentiment, had a beneficial effect on the country's modern art development. While Morocco's cultural heritage was largely unappreciated during the early part of the 20th century, it later became

45. Fatima Hassan al-Farouj
Untitled, 1989
Oil on canvas
31 1/2 x 39 1/2 in.
Collection of the artist

a source of inspiration for modern Moroccan artists.

During Spanish rule over the northern region of Morocco, several artists adopted academic and Postimpressionist styles. Their work was hardly recognized, however, because the Spanish colonial authorities encouraged only Orientalist and naive painting. After World War II an academic movement developed when the Escuela de Bellas Artes was established in 1945 in Tetouan, a part of the Spanish Protectorate. Immediately prior to Independence in 1956, contemporary Western styles began to appear in Morocco, propagated by the schools of fine art. With the opening of the Escuela de Bellas Artes in Tetouan and the École des Beaux Arts in Casablanca, the Orientalist school and naive painting began to lose their popularity. Emerging Moroccan artists began to turn to their roots for inspiration.

In the 1950s a few isolated painters such as Maḥjūbi Aherdane (b.1924), Aḥmad Sharqāwi (1934–1967) and Farīd Belkahia (b.1934) began experimenting to find a distinctive local style. Sharqāwi is noted as being the first avant-garde artist of Morocco's modern period. He went first to Paris to train at the École des Métiers d'Art, then enrolled in the École Nationale des Beaux Arts, and later finished his studies at the Academy of Fine Arts in Warsaw. Upon his return from Poland he was sent to Paris on a UNESCO scholarship to research Arabic calligraphy and symbols in Berber art. In the 1960s Sharqāwi became the first Moroccan artist to study seriously the significance of symbols and motifs found in tattoos, pottery, jewelry, rugs and leatherwork from across the Atlas Mountains and other parts of the country. When he included these in his art, he did not simply copy traditional symbols but graphically explored their shapes to give a new, mystical dimension to the composition. For Sharqāwi, color was as important as his symbols. He was the first Moroccan artist to develop his own abstract style, simultaneously Western and indigenous. Sharqāwi and his contemporaries of the 1950s established the framework upon which the Moroccan modern art movement would develop. Esteemed as pioneers, they were instrumental in accelerating the emergence of the modern art movement from the 1960s onwards. Their groundbreaking efforts were contemporaneous with the literary movement that reflected the same search for an authentic Moroccan identity.

In the 1960s the number of students sent abroad on scholarships increased, as did cultural exchanges between Morocco and Europe. Young painters became preoccupied with the concept of creating a modern perspective that would foster an independent national identity to interact with the Arab world, in particular, and the developing nations, in general. All artists emerging after independence received either all or part of their training in the West. They sought a national artistic identity that would incorporate both their Moroccan heritage and Western art techniques.

During the same period the illiterate naive painter Chaibia Tallal (b. 1929) emerged on the art scene. A self-taught artist from the country, she began painting with house paints, creating dreamlike shapes in primary colors that expressed her personal impressions of her immediate environment. She was "discovered" by Aḥmad Sharqāwi and Pierre Gaudibert, director of the Musée d'Art Moderne de la Ville de Paris. In 1966 the first exhibition of her work took place in a group show at the Musée d'Art Moderne.

The International Meeting of Artists (Rencontre internationale des artistes) which took place in Rabat during December 1963 and January 1964 was a landmark event. It succeeded in bringing together such famous artists as Picasso, Henri Matisse and Joan Miró, along with a number of internationally unrecognized Moroccan artists. This gathering became a stepping stone for Moroccan artists, facilitating their entry into the international arena. It not only established direct contact between local and world-renowned artists but also, for the first time, created an opportunity for dialogue between Arab and Western painters. The meeting convinced Moroccan artists that to be contemporary did not mean abandoning their own heritage, and they acknowledged that modern art perspectives could blend harmoniously with Islamic aesthetics.

Moroccan art illustrates how the development of contemporary Arab art follows a dual track—drawing on the richness of Arabic artistic traditions while fully participating in Western trends. Through their experimentation with calligraphy and the numerous written Berber characters and folk motifs, Moroccan artists succeeded in establishing a distinctive modern artistic language that is unrestricted by academic precepts.

Syria

By the 20th century Syrian artists had moved away from traditional practices of painting murals, creating book illustrations and decorating the surfaces of objects such as lamps, vases and other utensils. Free-standing easel painting had gradually become the norm. A Western-style art movement started much later in Syria than in Lebanon, and it took about four decades to gain momentum. Two schools influenced Syria's earliest known Western-style painters—the classical Ottoman style of copying nature and Orientalism. At times the two fused into an early type of Syrian representationalism. The best-known artist since the Ottoman period was Tawfīq Ṭāriq (1875–1945). The first Syrian artist to use oil paints, he became famous among high officials, who paid him handsomely for their portraits.

Syrian art circles were profoundly affected by French Orientalist painting and Impressionism during the years between 1920 (when Syria came under the French Mandate) and 1946 (when the country gained its independence). Introduced by visiting French artists, Orientalism portrayed historical events with particular emphasis on detail. Impressionism took artists out of their studios into nature, where they focused on color and light. It reached Syria through local artists who had gone to Europe on scholarship, as well as through visiting foreign artists.

One of the first artists to free Syrian painting from its blind imitation of nature in his search for an individual style was Sa'īd Taḥsīn (1904–1986). Taḥsīn was a self-taught artist who, as a child, had witnessed the ravages of the great famine that plagued Damascus between 1914 and 1918. This catastrophe, which moved him deeply, later was reflected in his work. His subjects were divided between genre scenes—cityscapes of old Damascus with its narrow streets and traditional houses, popular wedding ceremonies and episodes of daily life—and historic and humanitarian themes. The latter category included paintings of the battles of Yarmuk and Qadissiya, the founding of the Arab League and scenes of hunger and poverty. Taḥsīn's narrative style, with its bright impressionistic colors, had a naive quality attributed to his lack of formal training. He paid little attention to perspective, concentrating instead on the sound construction of the composition.

The most prominent early Impressionist in Syria was Michel Kirsheh (1900–1973). Kirsheh was a prolific artist who traveled to Paris and was greatly influenced by French Impressionism, adopting the style for his depictions of Damascus. Returning to Syria, he taught Impressionism in secondary schools, leaving an indelible imprint on a generation of students. Most of the artists who were active between the world wars studied in Paris or Rome, returning home with a purely academic background. Those who embraced Impressionism did so at a time when it was already on the wane in the West.

Prior to World War II, Mussolini's government offered Syrian students a group scholarship to study art in Italy. The Italian government hoped to disseminate Italian culture in Syria. This tactic was not welcomed by the French authorities, however, and they put a halt to all further scholarships. In 1938 the first group of students returned from Italy just as the government sent a second group to Egypt for art training. Members of both groups became art instructors and were instrumental in shaping the modern art movement in Syria. Until the end of the 1930s, Syria produced a limited number of painters.

The long years of World War II brought suffering from severe rationing of food and other materials, while internal resistance to French occupation became increasingly violent. Preoccupied with the horrors of war, the public was indifferent to the development of modern art. Contemporary artists worked under difficult conditions, without public support. Those who persevered did so purely out of dedication to their profession. This was not a period of high experimentation; realism and figuration were the most common styles. With the end of the war came improved conditions, accented by a major exhibition of the Paris School at the Institut Laique in Damascus in 1948. The exhibition included works by Picasso, Amedeo Modigliani and Kees Van Dongen and helped to increase Syrian artists' exposure to trends in Western modernism.

The end of France's mandate over Syria in 1946 marked the beginning of an active phase of the modern art movement, which witnessed rapid development in the plastic arts. New talent started to appear after the war. Emerging artists concentrated on local subjects and indigenous qualities, fostering a closer rapport with the public. Though the prevalent style

46. Rima Mardam-Bey
Dreams 2
1991
Charcoal and acrylic
61 x 34 in.
Collection of the artist

was still Impressionism, it developed local characteristics through artists' choices of subject matter. Popular themes included scenes of the countryside and the old quarters of Damascus and other cities. While some artists experimented with Surrealism, creating works of great depth and symbolism, this style was never widely accepted; realism continued to dominate the art scene.

Syria's art movement was infused with renewed momentum in the 1950s with the emergence of a second generation of modern artists, most of whom had received their training in Egypt and Italy. While they devoted themselves to developing individual styles, they also worked as teachers, passing on their knowledge and experience to Syrian students. It was through the creative efforts of this group that the modern art movement moved beyond its former dependence on realism, with its narrow academic perspective, to an advanced level of awareness which encouraged the reconstruction of Syria's own cultural identity.

After the Suez War of 1956, Syrian artists began to search for new styles through which to confirm their national identity and artistic individuality. In 1958 a union between Syria and Egypt was declared (1958–1961). Gamal Abdel Nasser's call for opposition to the West had already found a strong response at almost every level of Syrian society. While artists began to reject Western art and look to their Arab-Islamic heritage for ways of expressing their political and social views, they also realized that modern art trends could be linked to their own artistic traditions. Inspired by Western artists such as Matisse and Paul Klee, who had rebelled against their own classical art teachings, the heritage-revival movement picked up momentum. This new trend, coupled with the political events and the general mood of the country, induced artists to develop distinctive styles that led in several new directions.

The early 1960s generated a young group of artists whose audacious experimentation enriched the modern art movement, opening new horizons for those who followed. At this stage in the development of Syria's modern art, Impressionism was in decline, and two new styles gained predominance—the first was a combination of expressionism and Abstract Expressionism; the second, abstractionism. Artists who pursued expressionism employed forms borrowed from their pre-Islamic classical heritage, reintroducing them in a modern Western style. In depicting the political and social upheavals rife in Syria and the Arab world, they used strong colors and distorted figuration to capture the general mood of the country and establish a rapport with the public. With its power to convey strong emotion, expressionism continues to be popular among Syrian artists.

The second major trend in Syrian art was abstractionism. Drawing mainly on calligraphy, it moved away from the personal and nationalistic tones common in expressionism. This new school was championed by Maḥmūd Hammād (1922–1988), the first Syrian artist to abstract Arabic letters and include them in compositions as structural elements.

Yet, whatever modern style Syrian artists espoused, their search for cultural continuity brought them back to the land itself. Whenever Syrian artists have sought their identity, they have invariably returned to an exploration and celebration of their surroundings which, in their eyes, represent the eternal connections between past and present. As one of the most ancient Arab cities, Damascus, with its old quarters, classical architecture and traditional character, always has held a strong appeal for artists, and modern artists are no exception. Painters have frequently portrayed the old quarters of Damascus, as well as Aleppo and other towns, since the beginning of the 20th century.

In the 1970s two different types of realism boldly emerged. Adherents of the first sensitively portrayed the local surroundings and archaeological sites in a detailed style that emphasized the beauty of the country. Artists in the second camp treated nationalistic and humanitarian subjects, such as war, aggression, poverty and oppression. They endeavored to establish a connection between image and reality through exaggeration, choosing to communicate ideas to their viewers rather than accurate visual records.

Jordan

Transjordan (modern Jordan) was founded in 1921 by Amīr 'Abd Allah, son of the Hashemite leader of the Arab Revolt, Sharīf Ḥusain bin 'Ali of Mecca. Like Palestine and Iraq, Transjordan became part of the British Mandate in 1922, while Lebanon and Syria were mandated to France. The country faced the formidable task of building a modern infrastructure with limited natural resources. Upon its independence in 1948, the Emirate of Transjordan became the Hashemite Kingdom of Jordan.

During the Ottoman era Jordan's population was a mixture of nomadic Bedouins, peasants and townspeople. Its indigenous art forms were limited to local handicrafts, including textile and rug weaving, embroidery, niello on silver (introduced by the Circassian émigrés), goldsmithing, pottery making, painting on glass, woodcarving and calligraphy. Hardly any traces of Western art existed in the country before the 1930s.

In the 1920s and 1930s a few foreign artists emigrated to Transjordan. It was through them that the first seeds of modern art were sown. Foremost among these pioneers were the Lebanese artist 'Umar Onsi (1901–1969), the Turkish painter Ziya'al-dīn Sulaiman (1880–1945) and the Russian artist George Aleef (1887–1970). Their greatest contribution to Jordan's modern art movement was their effectiveness in introducing Western-style painting to the public and their success in cultivating an appreciation for new art among their friends and acquaintances.

At the outset of the first Arab-Israeli war and the creation of the State of Israel in 1948, hundreds of thousands of Palestinian refugees poured into Jordan during the first few weeks of fighting. They were followed by thousands more, all in need of housing, basic services, employment and schooling. Jordan had to cope overnight with a population that had almost doubled. The country had only its meager resources and limited foreign aid on which to depend.

The annexation of the West Bank—that part of Palestine not occupied by Israel—to Jordan in 1949 joined the fate of the two peoples living on either side of the River Jordan. Among the refugees were many Palestinian artists who were given Jordanian citizenship. Other artists were born to parents of Palestinian origin living in Jordan. This blending of the two cultures made it difficult to clearly differentiate between the Jordanian and Palestinian art movements from the 1950s onward. West Bank artists came to Amman to exhibit their

work, and Palestinian artists were employed by the Ministry of Education as art teachers at government schools and teacher training colleges. The Jordanian government also provided some Palestinian artists with scholarships to study in Italy, England and France. Even after Israel's occupation of the West Bank in 1967 and the declaration of an independent Palestinian government in 1988, many artists of Palestinian origin have chosen to be recognized as Jordanian citizens.

Early Jordanian artists of the post-1948 period were all self-taught amateurs who took up painting as a hobby. The first exhibitions of their art presented in the 1950s were organized by literary clubs. By the mid-1950s, however, students were being sent abroad for professional training. Returning from Europe in the early 1960s, they infused Jordan's art scene with fresh insights. The leading modern painter at this time was Muhanna Durrah (b. 1938), who graduated from the Accademia di Belle Arti in Rome in 1958. A gifted, prolific and temperamental artist, he established his own distinctive style at an early stage in his career. His highly expressive, monochromatic portraits and his fractured landscapes with cubist undertones revealed his dexterity at manipulating color and tonality and distributing mass. Durrah was the only local painter at the time to cultivate his own students, opening a studio in Amman, where he trained a number of young artists. Even today, elements of his style can still be detected in other artists' works.

After completing their training abroad, a second group of artists returned to Amman in the mid-1960s. Unlike the initial group who studied in Europe, most of the young artists of the 1960s received their training at Arab art colleges and academies in Baghdad, Cairo and Damascus. They later went on to either Europe or the United States for their postgraduate studies. Upon their return to Jordan they taught at the Institute of Fine Arts, government secondary schools or the Department of Fine Arts that was later established at Yarmouk University.

In June of 1967, however, the second Arab-Israeli war abruptly halted this period of thriving artistic activity. In five days Israel occupied the Sinai and Jordan's West Bank, dividing both the land and its people. West

47. Khairat al-Saleh
The Creation 2
Gouache, gold leaf
and ink on paper
18 x 27 ½ in.
Collection Suha Shoman

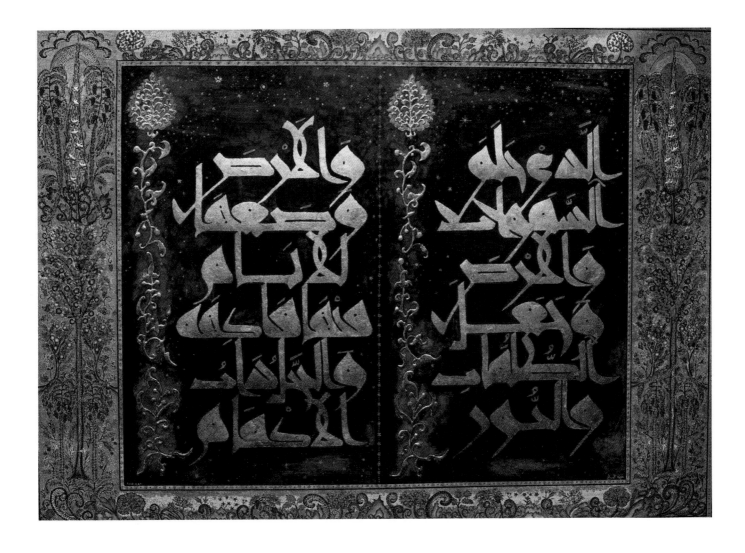

Bank artists were cut off from Jordan, and some emigrated to Europe and the United States. This military defeat and political setback instigated a wave of pessimism among the artistic and literary circles of the Arab world. The works created at this time revealed the bitterness and disappointment artists and intellectuals felt toward their leadership. They also carried a nationalistic message opposing the Israeli occupation. It is hardly surprising that the pace of artistic development in Jordan slowed considerably between 1967 and 1970, given the harsh political and economic realities the country faced during these years.

The modern art movement began to stir once again in the early 1970s. The appointment of Muhanna Durrah to the directorship of the Department of Arts and Culture in 1971 was a boon to Jordan's art world. He founded the Institute of Fine Arts, which employed noted artists as teachers, including Durrah himself. These teachers nurtured a number of second-generation artists, some of whom continued their studies in Europe, but returned to establish their place within Jordan's artistic community. Their painting styles varied, and they expressed themselves through individual approaches that moved between expressionism and abstractionism. Their training, whether in Western or Arab academies, directed them toward current international styles. Like their counterparts in other Arab countries, these emerging artists were drawn to the land and to traditional elements. They used their depictions of local landscapes, folk motifs and calligraphy as a means of asserting a national artistic identity.

In 1975 Fahrelnissa Zeid (1901–1991), an artist of Turkish origin and a prominent figure in Turkish modern art, moved from Paris to Amman. She was married to the Hashemite Prince Zeid al-Ḥusain, the youngest son of Sharīf Ḥusain bin 'Ali of Mecca. She had studied at Istanbul's Academy of Fine Arts and the Académie Ranson in Paris. Zeid had spent most of her life between Berlin, London and Paris, accompanying her husband who was an ambassador of Iraq during the Hashemite monarchy. A seasoned and versatile artist, she opened a studio in Amman, the Royal Art Institute of Fahrelnissa Zeid, where she gave painting lessons to a group of women. Many of Zeid's students emulated her abstract style and Byzantine portraits. Two of her students, Suha Shoman and Hind Nasser, distinguished

themselves, becoming prominent artists in their own right.

In 1979 the Royal Society of Fine Arts was established in Amman as a private, nonprofit organization dedicated to the promotion of visual arts in Jordan and the Islamic world. In 1980 the society founded the Jordan National Gallery of Fine Arts, the first of its kind in the country. It is thus far the only art gallery in the world that collects works exclusively by Islamic artists and those of the developing nations. From its inception, the National Gallery set high standards for Jordanian artists through its discriminating choice of exhibitions and acquisitions. Its efforts made possible for the first time exhibitions of original works by established Western and Arab artists. The National Gallery has presented more than fifty major exhibitions from Europe and the Middle East, displaying works by leading contemporary artists, including Henry Moore, Barbara Hepworth, Maria Elena Vieira da Silva, Maḥmūd Mukhtār, Fā'iq Hassān and 'Umar Onsi. Its regular cultural activities have offered new perspectives to local artists and the general public. It has taken exhibitions to other Jordanian cities, and even to remote areas where villagers and Bedouins have been able to view Western-style paintings for the first time in their lives. Proud of the artistic achievements of the Arab world, the National Gallery also has been instrumental in introducing Jordanian and modern Islamic art abroad, traveling exhibitions from its permanent collection to Turkey, Poland, France, England, Egypt, Canada and Italy.

In 1989 the Royal Society of Fine Arts, in cooperation with the Islamic Arts Foundation in London, organized the largest exhibition of contemporary Islamic art yet held in the West. *Contemporary Art from the Islamic World* was presented at the Barbican Centre in London. It included 254 works by 107 artists from 19 Islamic countries, from Brunei to Morocco. The catalogue published to accompany the exhibition records the development of fine art in the countries represented.

Palestine
As late as 1948, "fine art" in the Western sense of the term had not yet fully developed in Palestine. Artists predominantly practiced traditional and folk arts and crafts, including embroidery, pottery making, weaving and straw work, calligraphy, icon painting, wood

48. Fahrelnissa Zeid
The Reverse
1964
Oil on canvas and wood
52 3/4 x 65 in.
Collection Errol Karim
Aksoy Foundation

49. Suha Shoman
Legend of Petra
1989
Triptych detail
Oil on canvas
79 x 59 in.
Collection of the artist

engraving, stone carving and mosaic and mother-of-pearl work.

When Palestine came under British rule in 1917, there was no immediate artistic renaissance. Unlike the French colonists, British Mandate authorities did little to further the cultural development of the countries they controlled. They were primarily interested in training qualified civil servants to work for the bureaucracy they established; art education and patronage were low on their list of priorities. Furthermore, the internal clashes between Arabs and Jews, coupled by uprisings and general strikes against the British, did little to encourage authorities to send students abroad on art scholarships or include art classes in school curricula.

Despite the difficulties, Palestinian artists nevertheless strove to enter the modern era. Noted among Palestine's pioneer generation are Hanna Musmar (1898–1988), considered the country's first modern artist, and Faddūl 'Awdah (b. 1906), the first Palestinian to study painting in Europe. 'Awdah traveled to Florence, not under the auspices of the British government but on a scholarship secured by an Italian priest from the Convent of Nazareth in 1922. Another early painter was Da'ūd Zalātīmo (b. 1906), who depicted historical events, famous monuments and landscapes. Working in situ, he used a simple, naive style that differed from that of the Orientalists.

Fāṭima Muhīb (b. 1920) was one of the first women from Palestine to formally study art. She graduated from the College of Fine Arts in Cairo in 1940 and obtained her master's in fine art from Helwân University in 1942. Other early women artists were Sofie Halaby from Jerusalem and Lydia Atta from Bethlehem. Halaby, who studied art in Paris, excelled in soft watercolors of Palestinian landscapes and detailed wild flowers. Atta painted scenes of churches and domes, but left few works behind when she emigrated to Australia in 1940.

Most early Palestinian artists were untrained amateurs. Those who were trained imitated the styles they were taught, executing works in oils, watercolors and pastels depicting landscapes, still lifes and portraits of historical and contemporary personalities and biblical themes. Not a single group or solo exhibition was held in Palestine before 1948.

Following the creation of the State of Israel in 1948, Palestinians, among whom were a small number of artists, were dispersed throughout the other Arab states. Some of these displaced artists became citizens of their adopted countries and were active in the art circles of their new homes. Others kept their national character despite the diaspora and have always been identified as Palestinians.

To examine the development of the Palestinian modern art movement since 1948, one has to deal with artists living in Israel and the Occupied Territories separately from those of the diaspora. The matter is complicated by the fact that Palestinian artists were uprooted several times, first in 1948 and then again in 1967. The outbreak of civil war in Lebanon in 1975, followed by the Israeli invasion of the country in 1982, prompted many Palestinians then living in Lebanon to move again.

Ismail Shammout (b. 1930) is considered to have been a leader of the modern art movement during the 1960s. A formally trained artist, he was the first to establish a content-oriented movement which focused on Palestinian subjects—specifically the suffering of the people and the loss of their motherland—and was the first to utilize those subjects in the service of his people's cause. Shammout's wife, Tamam al-Akhal (b. 1935), was the first Palestinian woman artist to acquire formal art training after 1948.

Circumstances for Palestinian artists improved considerably when the Gaza Strip came under Egyptian sovereignty in 1949. The government began to provide Gaza with art teachers and supplies, invigorating art education by providing professional training to talented youths. In Jordan, Lebanon and Syria, Palestinian students followed the governments' curricula, taking active roles in the art movements of each country. Between 1953 and 1965, about one hundred young Palestinian men and women, almost half of them from Gaza, pursued art studies at different institutions in Cairo, Alexandria, Baghdad, Damascus, London, Rome, Paris, Leipzig, Dresden, Tokyo, Washington and Madrid. Some were sent abroad on scholarships by Arab governments, while others financed their own studies.

Not much is known of Palestinian artists living in Israel between 1948 and 1955, probably because there was little artistic activity during that period. Among the Palestinian artists living in Israel today is As'ad 'Izzi (b. 1955), a painter and sculptor who graduated from the Accademia di Belle Arti in Carrara, Italy, and from Tel Aviv University. Another artist is 'Abd 'Abīdī, who executed a monument in bas-relief with the Israeli artist Kershon Kensbil which depicted Palestinians' attachment to the land. Other artists studied art in occupied Jerusalem, Haifa and abroad, although little is known of their activities.

Since 1967 the work produced under occupation reveals anger and resentment. Working under difficult and sometimes extremely disruptive conditions, artists have attempted to express their defiance through their art. Those living in the West Bank and Gaza Strip have had to resort to nonaggressive, artistic expressions of nationalism to be able to display their work without incurring the wrath of the occupying authorities, who banned the use of the colors of the Palestinian flag (black, red, green and white) in art.

In 1964 the Palestinian Liberation Organization (PLO) was formed. Ismail Shammout was appointed Director of Arts for the PLO in Beirut, thereby giving Palestinian artists the official patronage they lacked. He has since organized numerous exhibitions in the Arab world and abroad, using art to advance the Palestinian cause.

A form of expression particular to Palestinian artists is prison art. Among the thousands who have been put behind bars by the occupying authorities, a few have taken up painting. Using white handkerchiefs and colored crayons smuggled into prison, these prisoner-artists create emotionally charged compositions that cannot be assigned to any particular style. Simultaneously realistic, symbolic, surrealistic, expressionistic and naive, the works are no larger than 12 × 12 in., the size of a handkerchief—the only material available for painting in prison. All the prison artists are serving life sentences and live under great duress. Just as their materials are smuggled into prison, their work is smuggled out. They use limited colors and depend on symbolism to express their anger and frustration. One of their main symbols is the Palestinian flag, which is included in most of the works.

Many of the Palestinian artists dispersed throughout the world have succeeded in establishing careers in their new places of residence. While many early artists employed the elements of traditional Islamic and local crafts which had such a potent influence on art in Palestine through the 1950s, Western-style painting and sculpture have become the norm. The plight of the Palestinian people has resulted in four groups of artists: those living in Israel; those living under occupation; those residing in other Arab countries; and the group dispersed in Europe, the United States and Asia. Whether directly or indirectly, they have all experienced the existential stress created by the political realities of their homeland. They are thus all united by their subject matter, which revolves around the political and social issues linked with the loss of their nationhood. Even those born outside Palestine and integrated into the art movements of their host countries have demonstrated strong national bonds. They frequently visit their families in the Occupied Territories and Israel, creating content-oriented art that deals with the difficulties faced by their people. This obsession with one's country, which is unique in the history of Arab art, has affected other Arab artists, as well as Israeli artists. For Palestinian artists, their work has become a passionate and introspective means of safeguarding their identity and promulgating their cause throughout the world.

Sudan

Sudan became a political entity after the Turkish-Egyptian conquest of the region in 1821. No major cities existed in Sudan until the country gained independence from the British in 1951. The capital, Khartoum, was a British creation with a large foreign community, including British, Copts and Greeks. The country's cultural heritage is comprised of Egyptian, African, Coptic and Islamic elements. Modern art, specifically painting, is a recent phenomenon in Sudanese culture, only emerging in the 1940s. Nomadic crafts in leatherwork, metalwork, weaponry, weaving and jewelry were the most common forms of visual art, as no tradition of Islamic architecture or applied arts had ever developed in Sudan. Besides local handicrafts, poetry and music were the main forms of artistic expression. While calligraphy was practiced because of its bond to the Qur'ān, it never reached the level of sophistication attained in other Islamic countries.

In the 1920s poets dominated the Sudanese literary world. They were public orators and

50. Mona Saudi
Formation
1992
Limestone
15³/₄ x 12 x 4 in.
Collection of the artist
Photo by Kalle Hover

51. Samira Badran
United Fire
1993
Acrylic on paper
43 1/2 x 47 in.
Collection of the artist
Photo courtesy Jordan National
Gallery of Fine Arts

**52. Rima Farah
with Kevin Jackson
Pot, 1987
Etching
32 x 36 ½ in.
Collection Jordan National
Gallery of Fine Arts**

performers who delivered religious, historical, mystical and romantic messages extolling past glories. In their poems they portrayed an imagery that fused tradition with the force of drama. During the second half of the 1920s, untrained folk artists started to respond to this poetic imagery. They painted naive scenes of local girls and watermelons in primary colors, disregarding perspective, light and shade. Working with ordinary house paints and enamels for metal surfaces, they painted on wooden planks and on canvases of native cotton, which they stretched on wood frames.

In comparison to the early experiences of some of its neighbors, Sudan's formal introduction to Western art techniques came relatively late in its history. The Department of Education (later the Ministry of Education) sent the first group of art teachers abroad on scholarship in 1945. A second group followed in 1946, traveling to Egypt and England. The Sudanese search for a national artistic identity dominated the works of its early artists well before Western art styles became prevalent, unlike the pattern of development followed in other Arab countries. Because of the absence of an early Western art tradition in Sudan and the pervasive presence of indigenous handicrafts, local trends in art predominated Sudanese paintings of the 1940s and 1950s. Consequently, the works of the first generation of modern artists were imbued with an indigenous character, while international styles only appeared in the art of later generations.

Sudan's modern art movement gained momentum between 1950 and 1960, when three main art groups emerged. The most important was the Old Khartoum School, formed by a group of pioneer painters and sculptors who sought to discover a Sudanese identity through their work. The most prominent members of this school were 'Ushmān Waqīallah (b.1925), Ibrahim Salahi and Ahmad Shibrain. They blended African tribal designs with Arabic calligraphy and Islamic arabesque, using modern techniques to create an indigenous Sudanese style of art.

The adherents of the second group, the New Khartoum School, borrowed less from Sudan's cultural past, claiming to be more Western in their use of media and technique. Yet, in reality, the Old and New Khartoum Schools were rather similar, with the exception that works of the Old School exhibited more depth and

spontaneity. Despite their professed Western bent, artists of the New School did employ Sudanese imagery, as well as local art forms, such as basketry and collage.

The third Sudanese school, called the Crystalists, was the only group to publish a manifesto. The Crystalists most closely followed Western art styles, shunning influences from Sudan's cultural past. One of its main figures, Kamala Ibrahim Isahag, was also a member of the Old Khartoum School.

The Arabian Peninsula

At the start of the 20th century, Arabia—which includes the states of Saudi Arabia, Kuwait, Qatar, Bahrain, the United Arab Emirates, Oman and Yemen—remained in a geographically isolated position, far from any outside cultural influences. The people of the peninsula satisfied their need for artistic expression through crafts, the most common of which were weaving; embroidery; silver and gold jewelry-making; woodcarving; and naive, two-dimensional, decorative paintings on boats, walls and the doors of houses and mosques. Craftspeople found inspiration for their designs, choice of color and subject matter in their environment, borrowing little from outside sources. On the coasts, foreign influence came mainly from the East—the Indian subcontinent and its islands—as evidenced by imports of glass and pottery. Local crafts, however, declined once oil was discovered. As the interests of the Western powers in the Arabian Peninsula rose, cars and cement became central to the lives of the people.

Three factors were instrumental in introducing Western art to the Arabian Peninsula—the educational system, the availability of scholarships and the formation of art societies. Western art concepts first penetrated Arabia in the 1950s through the modern educational system. Although modern schools were sporadically founded as early as 1912 in Kuwait, 1919 in Bahrain, 1925 in Saudi Arabia and 1926 in Oman, the most common system of education in Arabia until the 1930s was the traditional *kuttab*. A group of young children would assemble around a tutor, in his house or in the mosque, to memorize the Qur'ān and learn discipline and good manners. A modern educational system gradually replaced the traditional one and, by the 1950s, schools teaching a variety of subjects became the norm. These modern schools also assumed additional roles,

53. Nabila Hilmi
People Series
1993
Mixed media on paper
9 x 12 in. each
Collection of the artist

becoming community centers for social and cultural activities, public gatherings, sporting events, plays and exhibitions. The school also became a playground for children, replacing the village square. The classroom became the center of their artistic activities, where they were given art instruction which conformed to the country's Department of Education programs. The Department of Education in Saudi Arabia and the other Gulf countries, for instance, introduced drawing and painting lessons to their curricula. An innovator in the field of education, Kuwait became the first country in the region to implement a modern school system in 1936, and the first to grant scholarships in the arts (which makes its modern art movement the oldest among those in the peninsula). In the 1940s Kuwait became the first country to include art education in its curriculum. After Kuwait, Saudi Arabia was one of the first countries in the region to understand the importance of art education.

Scholarships granted by governments constitute the second element that helped to introduce Western art trends into the region, as educational authorities in Saudi Arabia and the Gulf started sending students abroad to study art. The first art scholarship recipient from the peninsula was the Kuwaiti Mujab Dussari (1921–1956), who was sent to the Institute of Decorative Arts in Cairo. Bahrain, Saudi Arabia, Qatar and the United Arab Emirates sent art students to England, Iraq, Italy, Egypt and Syria. Over the years, the number of art students studying outside the peninsula has steadily increased. Returning home, they share their new knowledge and experience, adding fresh perspectives to their countries' evolving art movements.

The formation of art societies in Arabia has played a significant role in the development of its modern art movement. The earliest societies were established in Kuwait and Saudi Arabia (1967); other countries, such as Qatar, the United Arab Emirates and Oman soon followed suit. All of these societies, whether publicly or privately established, receive official subsidies and have been instrumental in furthering the arts. They arrange exhibitions at home and abroad, establish contacts with other Arab and international artistic institutions, establish collections of works by local artists, award prizes in the fine arts and spread artistic awareness among the public. Members

of artistic groups are not bound by a certain style or school. In their own way, these societies assume a role similar to that of artists' associations and unions in other countries. They are a combination of art fraternity, art institute, artists' union and government cultural department.

A new phenomenon which appeared on the Arab art scene in 1960 was the Free Atelier for Fine Arts in Kuwait. Providing studio space and art materials, the Atelier offers art classes for national and foreign-resident art students. The Kuwait Department of Education (later the Ministry of Education) opened the Free Atelier as a nucleus for an arts college. In its early stages, the Free Atelier only accepted male students. It offered classes in painting, sculpture and printmaking both during the day and in the evening, enabling a wide range of students and artists to attend. Filling a great need in the artistic community, the Atelier was an immediate success, despite the fact that it did not offer a certificate. In 1972 the Atelier became the responsibility of the Ministry of Information (which was transformed into the governing authority for all artistic and cultural affairs in Kuwait) and was transferred to a new location in a traditional Kuwaiti house. At this point it became a publicly supported studio, intended strictly for the benefit of Kuwaiti artists. The first instructors at the Free Atelier were art teachers from the Department of Education. Established Kuwaiti artists later took over all teaching responsibilities.

The great success of the Free Atelier surpassed the expectations of its founders and sponsors. Following Kuwait's lead, Qatar opened a Free Atelier in Doha in 1980. In the same year Oman started the Atelier of Plastic Arts in Muscat.

A second progressive program, which began in Kuwait in 1961, is the state support of full-time artists. Providing artists with a monthly salary for two or more years, this program enables them to fully dedicate themselves to their creative pursuits.

Despite the social restrictions imposed on women in Arabia, a considerable number, mainly painters, have established themselves as artists. Among them are Thuraya al-Baqsami from Kuwait, whose two-dimensional

54. Suad al-Attar
Legend I
1991
Oil on canvas
72 x 60 in.
Collection of the artist

paintings are inspired by classical Islamic miniatures; Mounirah Mosly from Saudi Arabia, who explores subjects relating to feminist issues; and Nadira Mahmoud from Oman, who paints totally abstract compositions.

Paintings produced during the 1950s and 1960s throughout the Arabian Peninsula can be characterized by their primitive figurative style. Artists at this time adhered to no consistent art school, depicting their subjects realistically in primary colors. The increase in the number of government scholarships, along with the ensuing exposure to Western art, led to a departure from the old, rather rigid subject matter to a new era of experimentation with different Western art schools. The most popular styles of painting have been Impressionism, Abstract Expressionism, Cubism and Surrealism. In the 1960s the Kuwaiti 'Abd Allah Taqi was the first artist in the area to depart from academic restrictions and turn to abstraction.

As in other Islamic countries, a considerable number of painters incorporate Arabic letters and Islamic arabesque motifs in their works. Regardless of style and artistic level, paintings by Gulf artists, whether of cities or landscapes, still lifes or portraits, realistic scenes or surrealistic images, have one common denominator—their choice of subject matter, taken from scenes of everyday life and indigenous culture. The first painter to focus on local subjects was the Kuwaiti Mujab Dussarī. Other early artists from the area followed his example. The most common subjects among painters are the sea, the desert and life in their own communities.

Long before oil was discovered, the sea and the desert isolated the people of the Arabian Peninsula, while remaining a source of inspiration for their poetry. With the discovery of oil, societies in the peninsula were suddenly exposed to fundamental social and economic changes at a more rapid pace than other Arab countries. The conservative communities that had been able to safeguard most of their customs and traditions for centuries started to lose their grip on the cohesion of their cultural continuity, particularly since oil brought them sudden and overwhelming affluence, as well as massive exposure to the technology and commercialism of Western civilization. Faced with this phenomenon, Arabian artists have made an attempt to preserve on canvas their old cultural traditions, recording for posterity those practices that are already disappearing or may well do so with time.

Conclusion

Although changes in the political, economic and social environment since the 19th century caused a decline in the traditional arts of the Arab world, these changes simultaneously paved the way for the development of a modern Arab art that encompassed Western aesthetics. Since the mid-19th century an artistic renaissance has developed in the Middle East and North Africa, leading to an artistic evolution in the field of visual arts, especially painting. By the mid-20th century nearly all of the Arab countries had modern art movements. The Arab world's cultural and artistic growth is clearly visible in the development of its arts institutions, the range of its artistic activities, the growing number of artists it nurtures and the level of sophistication these artists have achieved in their work.

55. Balqees Fakhro
Birth, 1992
Acrylic
30 x 30 in.
Collection of the artist

56. Ghada Jamal
To Everything There
Is a Season
1989
Artist's book,
mixed media
8 x 12 in.
Collection Dr. and Mrs.
Frank Agrama

Further Reading

English

Ali, Wijdan. *Contemporary Art from the Islamic World*. London, 1989.

Barbour, N., *Morocco*. London, 1965.

Contemporary Art in Kuwait. Kuwait, 1983.

Julian, Phillipe. *The Orientalists: European Painters of Eastern Scenes*. Trans. from the French by Helga and Dinah Harrison. Oxford, England: Phaidon, 1977.

Karnouk, Liliane. *Modern Egyptian Art: The Emergence of a National Style*. Cairo: American University in Cairo Press, 1988.

Lahoud, Edouard. *Contemporary Art in Lebanon* (L'art contemporain au Liban). Adapt. in English by Philippe M. Michaux; adapt. in French by Rene Lavenant. New York: Near East Books, 1974; Beirut: Librarie Orientale, 1974.

Lebanon—The Artist's View: 200 Years of Lebanese Art. Exhibition catalogue. London: Barbican Centre, 1989.

French

Fazekas, S., *La Villa Abd-El-Tif et ses Peintres (1907-1962)*. Paris: Mémoire de Maitrise, n.d.

Musées d'Algerie II - L'Art Algerien Populaire et Contemporain. Madrid: Collection "Art et Culture," 1973.

La Peinture Européenne en Tunisie sous le Protectorat. Catalogue d'exposition. Tunis: Centre d'Art Vivant de la Ville de Tunis, 1989.

La Peinture en Tunisie des Origines a nos Jours. Catalogue d'exposition. Tunis: Centre d'Art Vivant de la Ville de Tunis, n.d.

Salim, N. *L'Art Contemporain en Iraq*. Lausanne, 1977.

Sijelmassi, M. *L'Art Contemporain au Maroc*. Paris, 1989.

Arabic

Bahnasī, 'Afīf "Taṭawur al-fann al-sūrī khilāl mi'at 'ām" (The development of Syrian art throughout a hundred years) *Al-hawliyāt al-'athariyah al-'arabiyah al-sūrīyah (HAAS)* 23, nos. 2 and 3 (1973): 11-24.

———. *Al-fann al-ḥadīth fi' al-bilād al-'arabiyah* (Modern art in the Arab countries). Tunis, 1980.

———. *Ruwwād al-fann al-ḥadīth fi' al-bilād al-'arabiyah* (Pioneers of modern art in the Arab countries). Beirut, 1985.

Iskandar, I., K. Mallakh and S. Sharuni. *Thamānūna sana min al-fann* (Eighty years of art). Cairo, 1991.

Al-Sa'īd, S. H. *Fuṣul min tarīkh al-ḥaraka al-tashkīliyah fi'l-'Irāq - juzu' awwal* (Chapters from the art movement in Iraq). Baghdad, 1983.

Salmān, A. *Al-tashkīl al-mu'aṣir fī duwal majlis al-ta'āwun al-khalījī* (Modern art in the countries of the Gulf Cooperation Council). Kuwait, 1984.

Shammout, Ismail. *Al-fann al-tashkīlī fī filistīn* (Palestinian art). Kuwait: Al-Qabas Press, 1989.

Mariam A. Aleem

Born Alexandria, Egypt. Received her B.A. in 1954 and M.F.A. in 1975 from University of Southern California and Ph.D. in fine arts from the University of Helwân in Egypt. Also studied fine arts at the Pratt Institute in New York. In 1968 Aleem became a professor at the Department of Printed Design in the Faculty of Fine Arts, Alexandria. She was appointed director of the faculty in 1981.

Aleem has had solo exhibitions in United States, Lebanon, Egypt, Germany, Italy and Norway. In addition to the Selected Group Exhibitions listed below, the artist also has participated in group shows in France, Luxembourg, India, China, the United States, the United Kingdom, Iraq, Kuwait and Yemen.

Her prizes and awards include: first prize, Biennial Norwegian Festival (1954); National Award from Egypt (1973); the National Order for Art and Science of the First Degree from Egypt (1974); award, International Year of the Woman from Egypt and Italy (1975); first prize, Biennial Norwegian Festival (1984); and Graphics arts prize at the Graphics Biennial in Norway (1986 and 1989).

Selected Group Exhibitions:
1954 Biennial Norwegian Festival
1957 Alexandria Biennial, Alexandria, Egypt
1961 Alexandria Biennial, Alexandria, Egypt
1963 Ljubljana Biennial, Ljubljana, Yugoslavia
1964 Venice Biennial, Venice, Italy
1965 Alexandria Biennial, Alexandria, Egypt
1969 Ljubljana Biennial, Ljubljana, Yugoslavia
1984 Biennial Norwegian Festival
     International Exhibition of Graphics, Yokohama, Japan
1985 International Exhibition of Graphics, Yokohama, Japan
1986 São Paulo Biennial, São Paulo, Brazil
     Graphics Biennial, Norway
     Kraków Biennial, Kraków, Poland
1987 International Graphics Exhibition, East Germany
1989 Ljubljana Biennial, Ljubljana, Yugoslavia
     Graphics Biennial, Norway
1990 International Graphics Exhibition, Russia
1991 Triennial, Finland
     Ljubljana Biennial, Ljubljana, Yugoslavia
1994 *Forces of Change: Artists of the Arab World*, The National Museum of Women in the Arts, Washington

Ivonne A-Baki

A-Baki is a Lebanese artist born in Ecuador in 1951. She trained at the University of Beirut in architecture and also established a successful career in the foreign service. Served as Artist-in-Residence at Dudley House, Harvard University, and has recently earned her master's in public administration at Harvard's Kennedy School of Government. Many of her paintings are on permanent display at such institutions as the presidential palaces of Lebanon and Ecuador, as well as in various international museums.

Selected Solo Exhibitions:
1981 German Cultural Center, Beirut, Lebanon
1982 Unicentro de las Americas, Guayaquil, Ecuador
1984 Galerie Katia Granoff, Paris
1985 Galerie Katia Granoff, Cannes, France
1987 The International Monetary Fund, Washington
1988 Keith Green Gallery, New York
1989 Museo Nacional Benjamin Carrión, Quito, Ecuador
1990 Dudley House, Harvard University, Cambridge, Mass.
     Whig Hall, Princeton University, Princeton, N.J.
1992 The Cathedral of St. John The Divine, New York

Selected Group Exhibitions:
1984 Art Festival '84, Beiteddeen, Beirut, Lebanon
1985 Festival of Graphic Arts, Osaka, Japan
1985 American Academy, Paris
     Art Festival '85, Beiteddeen, Beirut, Lebanon
1986 Art Festival '86, Beiteddeen, Beirut, Lebanon
1987 Art Festival '87, Beiteddeen, Beirut, Lebanon
1994 *Forces of Change: Artists of the Arab World*, The National Museum of Women in the Arts, Washington

Amna Abdalla

Born in Sudan. Graduated from the National College of Art, Craft and Design in Stockholm, Sweden. Has exhibited extensively in Scandinavia. Received her master's degree in textile design and weaving. Apprenticed at Bayer of West Germany and at the Blue Nile Spinning and Weaving Factory in Khartoum, Egypt.

Abdalla has produced a series of television programs, educational workshops and post-graduate curricula in Saudi Arabia and Sudan. She lectures at King Faisal University in Dhahran, Saudi Arabia, and manages an interior design consulting firm. Recently she has come to the United States to study pottery.

Selected Solo Exhibitions:
1988/
1993 The Eman Gallery, al-Khubar, Saudi Arabia (yearly)
1989 The Youth Welfare Presidency Hall, Dammam, Saudi Arabia
     The Diplomatic Quarters of Rizayat Women's Center, Riyadh, Saudi Arabia
1990 ARAMCO, Dhahran, Saudi Arabia
1991 Panache Gallery, Dhahran, Saudi Arabia
1992 Panache Gallery, Dhahran, Saudi Arabia

1993 *Fingerprint* (with Mounirah Mosly),
Jedda, Saudi Arabia

Selected Group Exhibitions:
1988 The Jordan National Gallery, Amman,
Jordan
1989 The Bahrain Arts Society, Bahrain
The Dammam Municipality Sculpture
Exhibition, Dammam, Saudi Arabia
1992 Saudi Airlines, Jedda, Saudi Arabia
1993 al-Khubar, Saudi Arabia
1994 *Forces of Change: Artists of the Arab World*,
The National Museum of Women in
the Arts, Washington

Zeinab Abdel Hamid

Born in Cairo. Graduated in 1945 from Academy
of Fine Arts in Alexandria, Egypt. Graduate work
in Royal Academy of Fine Arts of San Fernando,
Madrid, Spain. Further studies in Mexico in 1964.
In 1969 she became a professor at the Academy
of Arts, Helwân, Egypt.

Abdel Hamid has been exhibiting her work since
1949 as a leading woman artist working in oil and
watercolors. One of the founders of the Modern
Arts Group in 1947, she has received many Egyptian and international awards and has represented
Egypt in numerous international exhibitions since
1950. She was commissioned to paint a large-scale
work for the *al-Ahrām* newspaper building. Her
art is found in many public locations in Egypt, as
well as in private collections in Egypt, Germany,
the United States, France, Spain and Mexico.

In addition to the selected exhibitions listed
below, the artist also has had solo exhibitions in
Madrid, Spain, from 1970 through 1972, and has
participated in group exhibitions in Poland, China,
Bahrain, Greece, Bulgaria, Italy, Qatar, Kuwait
and India.

Selected Solo Exhibitions:
1952 Arts Institute, Madrid, Spain
Organization of Supporters of the Arts,
Cairo, Egypt

Selected Group Exhibitions:
1947 Museum of Modern Art, Cairo, Egypt
1948 Museum of Modern Art, Cairo, Egypt
1949 Pavillon des Arts, Paris
1950 Venice Biennial, Venice, Italy
1953 São Paulo Biennial, São Paulo, Brazil
1954 Galerie André Moris, Paris
1975 Ten Leading Women Pioneers,
Cairo, Egypt
1976 *Five Egyptian Artists*, International Monetary
Fund, Washington
1994 *Forces of Change: Artists of the Arab World*,
The National Museum of Women in
the Arts, Washington

Etel Adnan

Born in Lebanon in 1925. Studied philosophy at
the Sorbonne in Paris, the University of California,
Berkeley, and Harvard. Taught philosophy of art
at Dominican College of San Rafael, San Rafael,
California, and has presented courses, classes and
lectures at over forty universities and colleges
throughout the United States.

Adnan creates oils, ceramics and tapestry. She
has also written more than ten books of poetry
and fiction, including *Sitt Marie-Rose*, which has
been translated into six languages. She lives in
California, Paris and Lebanon.

Selected Solo Exhibitions:
1961 O'Hanlon Gallery-Studio, Mill Valley, Calif.
1963/
1969 Dominican College Gallery, San Rafael,
Calif. (yearly)
1964 Karmanduca Gallery, San Francisco, Calif.
1973 Dar el-Fan, Beirut, Lebanon
1977 Galerie la Roue, Paris
1978 Galerie l'Atelier, Rabat, Morocco
1982 El Sultan Gallery, Kuwait City, Kuwait
1983 Alif Gallery, Washington
1984/
1985 Perception Gallery, San Francisco, Calif.
1986 Marin County Civic Center, San Rafael,
Calif.
1987 Galerie Samy Kinge, Paris
1990 Kufa Gallery, London
1992 Gallery 50 × 70, Beirut, Lebanon

Selected Group Exhibitions:
1964 Mendocino Art Center, Mendocino, Calif.
1969 Town Gallery, New York
1972 Columbia University, New York
1974 Municipal Museum, Tokyo
Sursock Museum, Beirut, Lebanon
Stuttgart Museum, Stuttgart, Germany
1978 Espace Cardin, Paris
Musée du Luxembourg, Paris
1979 Museum of Modern Art, Tunis, Tunisia
L'Atelier, Rabat, Morocco
1980 Galerie Matisse, Vichy, France
Iraqi Cultural Center, London
Galerie de Seine, Paris
Centre d'Art Vivant, Tunis, Tunisia
1981 Centre Culturel Paul Eluard, Bezons,
France
1985 Maison de l'Artiste, Grenoble, France
1987 Centre Culturel du Havre, Le Havre,
France
1988 Musée de l'Institut du Monde Arabe, Paris
1989 Chelsea Manor Studios, London
Cultural Center of Riyadh, Riyadh,
Saudi Arabia
1990 Villa Croce, Genoa, Italy
1991 UNESCO, Paris
Midiathèque, Les Mureaux, France
L'Atelier, Rabat, Morocco
Musée de l'Institut du Monde Arabe, Paris

1994 *Forces of Change: Artists of the Arab World,*
      The National Museum of Women in
      the Arts, Washington

Tamam al-Akhal

Born in Palestine in 1935. Displaced three times—
in 1948 from Palestine, in 1982 from Lebanon
and in 1991 from Kuwait. Educated first in Jaffa,
then in Beirut, Lebanon, and finally at the Higher
Institute of Arts in Cairo, Egypt, receiving a diploma in 1957. Taught art at the Makassed Girls
College in Beirut from 1957 to 1960.

Al-Akhal is one of the first Palestinian women to
be formally trained in the fine arts. The expressive
content of her work is based on the tragedy of
Palestinian national life. She heads the Art and
Heritage section of the PLO's department of
Information and Culture. She is a member of the
General Union of Palestinian Artists and of the
General Union of Arab Artists. She has chosen to
exhibit her work jointly with that of her husband,
Ismail Shammout.

      Selected Joint Exhibitions
      (with Ismail Shammout):
1954 Cairo, Egypt (under the patronage of
      President Gamal Abdel Nasser)
1960/
1962 Beirut, Lebanon (yearly)
1964 Jerusalem; Nablus, Jordan; Pittsburgh, Pa.;
      New York; Washington; Philadelphia, Pa.;
      Detroit and Ann Arbor, Mich.; Chicago
      and Champaign, Ill.; Houston and Austin,
      Tex.; Los Angeles and San Francisco,
      Calif.
1965 Tripoli, Lebanon; Cairo, Egypt; Damascus,
      Syria; Kuwait City, Kuwait
1966 Kuwait City, Kuwait
      London and Birmingham, England
1968 Alexandria and Cairo, Egypt
1970 Beirut, Lebanon
1973 Beijing, China
1974 Tunis, Tunisia; Algiers, Algeria; Rabat,
      Morocco
1976 Berlin, Paris, Rome
1977 Vienna
1979 Berlin
1982 Beirut, Lebanon
1984 Kuwait City, Kuwait
1989 Kuwait City, Kuwait
1994 *Forces of Change: Artists of the Arab World,*
      The National Museum of Women in
      the Arts, Washington

Ida Alamuddin

Born Beirut, Lebanon, in 1947. Received her first
bachelor's degree in fine arts from Mills College
in California in 1981 and her second in illustration
from the San Francisco Academy of Art in 1984.
Alamuddin has recently become an active participant in group exhibitions. Lives and works in
London.

      Selected Solo Exhibitions:
1980 Christie's Education Gallery, London
1988 Smith's Gallery, London

      Selected Group Exhibitions:
1988 *Contemporary British Artists,* Mayor Gallery,
      London
      Drawing show, Thumb Gallery, London
      United Kingdom-Cleveland Drawing
      Biennial, traveled within England
      Arab Women Artists, Kufa Gallery, London
      Contemporary Lebanese Artists, Kufa Gallery,
      London
1989 Musée de l'Institut du Monde Arabe, Paris
      Lebanon: The Artists's View, Barbican Centre,
      London
1992 Malvern Open Drawing Competition,
      Malvern, England
      The Hunting Observer Art Prizes, London
1994 *Forces of Change: Artists of the Arab World,*
      The National Museum of Women in
      the Arts, Washington

Wijdan Ali

Born in Amman, Jordan, in 1939, where she now
resides. Received her B.A. in history from Beirut
University College in 1961, while studying art privately. Received a Ph.D. in Islamic art from the
University of London in 1993.

Wijdan concentrates much of her artistic effort on
themes of universal tragedy, particularly the tragic
events in Arab history which took place in Carbala
during the 7th century. In her art she develops the
traditions of Arabic calligraphy in a modern format
and forms part of the contemporary school of
Arabic calligraphic painting. Her work, which has
won awards in Belgium and France, is found in
museums and private collections internationally.

In 1989 Wijdan edited *Contemporary Art from the
Islamic World.* She is the director of the Jordan
National Gallery of Fine Arts, which she founded.

      Selected Solo Exhibitions:
1965 Woodstock Gallery, London
      Galerie Wirth, Berlin
      Le Centre Culturel Français, Amman,
      Jordan
1972 Galerías Melia, Madrid
1973 Thor Gallery, Louisville, Ky.
1979 Middle East Institute, Washington
1981 Fine Arts Council, Karachi, Pakistan
1992 *Wijdan and Franco de Courten,* Shoman
      Gallery, Amman, Jordan
1993 The Gallery, Amman, Jordan

      Selected Group Exhibitions:
1961 Jordanian Artists Exhibition, Amman
      Municipality, Amman, Jordan
1982 Jordanian Art Exhibition, Moscow
      Assila Art Exhibition, Assila, Morocco
      Four Artists from Jordan, The Wraxall
      Gallery, London

Arab Artists Exhibition, Centre d'Art Vivant
de la Ville de Tunis, Tunis, Tunisia
1983/
1984 Jordanian Contemporary Art, Ankara State
Museum, Ankara, Turkey (traveled to
Istanbul, Turkey)
1986 Cairo Biennial, Cairo, Egypt
Baghdad International Festival of Art,
Sadam Center for the Arts, Baghdad, Iraq
*La Vie Royale: L'Art Contemporain en
Jordaine,* Musée du Luxembourg, Paris
1989 *Contemporary Art from the Islamic World,*
Barbican Centre, London
1991 *An Artist's Point of View,* McIntosh Gallery,
Toronto, Canada
South of the World, Galleria Civica d'Arte
Contemporanea, Marsala, Italy
Baghdad International Festival of Art,
Saddam Center for the Arts, Baghdad,
Iraq
1992 Contemporary Jordanian Art, International
World Fair, Seville, Spain
1993 *Re-creations,* Le Centre Culturel Français,
Amman, Jordan
1994 *Forces of Change: Artists of the Arab World,*
The National Museum of Women in
the Arts, Washington

Sawsan Amer

Born in Egypt, where she now resides. Graduated
from the College of Art Education in 1957. Amer
is the director of the Art Research Unit at the
Academy of the Arts and a professor on the faculty
of art education. She has authored a book and
numerous articles on folk art. A distinguished
artist, she received the Cairo Salon Prize in 1973.
She participates in many group exhibitions, and
her work is in numerous private and public collections in Egypt.

Selected Solo Exhibitions:
1973 Egyptian Cultural Center, Paris
1983 Egyptian Academy, Rome
International Exhibition, Spoleto, Rome
1984 Egyptian Cultural Center, Paris
1994 *Forces of Change: Artists of the Arab World,*
The National Museum of Women in
the Arts, Washington

Evelyn Ashmalla

Born in Desouk, Egypt. Graduated from the
Faculty of Fine Arts in Alexandria in 1973. In 1971
she participated in a group exhibition in Desouk,
Egypt, and from 1973 to 1978 she exhibited in
group shows throughout her native land. Between
1979 and 1982 she participated in group exhibitions in Algeria. She is a founding member of the
Syndicate of Plastic Artists and a member of Cairo
Atelier. She is presently a technical specialist in
the General Organization of Cultural Palaces.

Selected Solo Exhibitions:
1985 Cairo Atelier, Cairo, Egypt
1986 Cairo Atelier, Cairo, Egypt
1987 Cairo Atelier, Cairo, Egypt
Spanish Cultural Center, Egypt
1989 Round Gallery, Syndicate of Plastic Artists,
Egypt
1990 Cairo Atelier, Cairo, Egypt

Selected Group Exhibitions:
1971 Two Artists, Desouk, Egypt
1984 Two Artists, Kafr el-Sheikh Cultural Palace,
Egypt
1987 Salon of the Society of Friends of Fine Arts,
Alexandria, Egypt
1988 Art against Oppression, Cairo Atelier, Cairo,
Egypt
1989 Cairo Atelier, Cairo, Egypt
1994 *Forces of Change: Artists of the Arab World,*
The National Museum of Women in
the Arts, Washington

Suad al-Attar

Born in Baghdad, Iraq, in 1942. Studied at the
California Polytechnic State University, San Luis
Obispo, and at the University of Baghdad in Iraq.
She received a graduate degree in printmaking
from Wimbledon School of Art in London and
another degree in printmaking from the Central
School of Art and Design in London.

Al-Attar was the first Iraqi woman artist to have
a solo exhibition in Baghdad. She has received
awards from many international biennials, including those in Cairo, Brazil, London, Madrid and
Poland. Her work is in museum collections internationally.

Selected Solo Exhibitions:
1965 Al-Wasiti Gallery, Baghdad, Iraq
1968 Gallery One, Beirut, Lebanon
1970 Alwiyah Gallery, Baghdad, Iraq
1973 National Museum of Modern Art, Baghdad,
Iraq
1974 Centre d'Accueil du Proche Orient, Paris
1981 Annexe Gallery, London
1983 Graffiti Gallery, London
1985 Alif Gallery, Washington
1989 The Artist's Studio, London
1990 Europa Galleries, Los Angeles

Selected Group Exhibitions:
1965 Gallery One, Beirut, Lebanon
1974 Triennial of International Art, New Delhi,
India
1978 Stowells Trophy Competition, Royal
Academy of Art, London
1982 International Print Biennial, Fredrikstad,
Norway
1984 Cairo Biennial, Cairo, Egypt
1985 International Print Biennial, Kraków, Poland
1987 *Arab Artists,* Mall Galleries, London
1988 International Biennial, Museum of Modern
Art, Baghdad, Iraq

1989 *Contemporary Art from the Islamic World*,
   Barbican Centre, London
1991 Summer Exhibition, Royal Academy of Art,
   London
1994 *Forces of Change: Artists of the Arab World*,
   The National Museum of Women in
   the Arts, Washington

Ginane Makki Bacho

Born in Beirut, Lebanon, in 1947, and now resides
near Washington. From 1975 to 1977 she studied
printmaking and fine arts at the Académie des
Beaux-Arts in Beirut, and in Chaville, France. She
received a bachelor's degree from Beirut University College in 1982, and a master of fine arts
degree from Pratt Institute in New York in 1987.

Bacho is a versatile artist who has taught both
printmaking and literature at the university level.
She has published her prints in book form. She
has received numerous awards and her work can
be found in several museum collections.

Selected Solo Exhibitions:
1983 Beirut University College, Beirut, Lebanon
1989 *Ginane Bacho: Recent Work*, Kufa Gallery,
   London

Selected Group Exhibitions:
1983 Salon de l'Académie des Beaux-Arts,
   Chaville, France
1984 Salon de la Gravure Originale, Musée de
   Bayeux, Bayeux, France
1985 *Arab Artists*, Alif Gallery, Washington, D.C.
   International Print Biennial, Rio de Janeiro,
   Brazil
   Representing the Self, 22 Wooster Gallery,
   New York
1986 *Field and Field, Seas and Seas*, Carolyn Hill
   Gallery, New York
1987 *Contemporary Lebanese Artists*, Kufa Gallery,
   London
   Small Worlds, 22 Wooster Gallery, New York
1988 *Coast to Coast*, Women's Caucus for Art
   (traveling exhibition)
1990 *Arab Women Artists*, Alif Gallery, Washington
   Book as Art III, Library and Research
   Center, The National Museum of Women
   in the Arts, Washington
   The Family, Nexus Gallery, Philadelphia, Pa.
1994 *Forces of Change: Artists of the Arab World*,
   The National Museum of Women in
   the Arts, Washington

Samira Badran

A Palestinian artist born in Tripoli, Libya, in 1954.
Studied painting and drawing at the Faculty of
Fine Arts at Cairo University in Egypt and continued her education at L'Accademia di Belle Arti in
Florence. There she received an additional degree
in etching and painting in 1982. She painted a
mural project at Liège University in Belgium in
1980. Badran's work is found in private and public
collections in Italy, Spain and Jordan.

Selected Solo Exhibitions:
1985 The Royal Cultural Center, Amman, Jordan
1987 Galería Piscolabis, Barcelona, Spain
   The British Council, Amman, Jordan
1992 Al-Fenix, Amman, Jordan

Selected Group Exhibitions:
1980 *Arab Women Artists*, Chelsea Library,
   London
   First National Art Exhibition for Arab
   Women Artists, Modern Art Gallery,
   Baghdad, Iraq
1982 Premi International de Dibuix Joan Miró,
   Barcelona, Spain
1983 Bagno a Ripoli, Florence, Italy
   Uno Spazio Per L'Arte, Comune di Busto
   Arsizio, Milan, Italy
1986 Salon del Tinell, Barcelona, Spain
   Door and Windows, Jerusalem
   L'Art Contemporain en Jordanie, Musée du
   Luxembourg, Paris
1988 *It's Possible*, The Great Hall Gallery,
   New York
1989 Havana Biennial, Havana, Cuba
   Can Xerracan, Motornes del Valles, Spain
1990 Centro Internazionale Multimedia, Salerno,
   Italy
1992 UNESCO Palace, Paris
   Sala Vincón, Barcelona, Spain
1994 *Forces of Change: Artists of the Arab World*,
   The National Museum of Women in
   the Arts, Washington

Thuraya al-Baqsami

Born in Kuwait in 1952. She was active as a teen-
ager in the Kuwait Formative Art Society. She
studied in London, Cairo and Dakar, Senegal.
In 1974 she earned her master's degree in book
illustration and design from the Arts Institute of
Surikow in Moscow. Al-Baqsami is a painter,
writer and illustrator who has won many awards
and contributes regularly to Kuwaiti magazines
and newspapers.

Selected Solo Exhibitions:
1978 Kinshasa, Zaire
1979 Free Art Gallery, Kuwait City, Kuwait
1982 Dakar, Senegal
1988 Ghadir Gallery, Kuwait City, Kuwait
1989 Montreux, Switzerland
1990 Ghadir Gallery, Kuwait City, Kuwait
1991 Kiklos Gallery, London
   Alpine Gallery, Kuwait City, Kuwait
   Ghadir Gallery, Kuwait City, Kuwait
1992 Athens College Theater, Athens

Selected Group Exhibitions:
1985 International Youth Festival, Moscow
   Riyadh, Saudi Arabia
1987 Madrid
1988 International Festival for Formative Arts,
   Baghdad, Iraq
1989 International Festival of Children's
   Illustration, Czechoslovakia

1989 *Contemporary Arab Art*, Islamic Cultural
    Center, London
1990 Bonn, Germany
    Washington
1992 National Museum, Kuwait City, Kuwait
    (first prize)
    Albert Gallery, London
1994 *Forces of Change: Artists of the Arab World*,
    The National Museum of Women in
    the Arts, Washington

Meriem Bouderbala
Born in Tunis in 1960. Studied etching and
painting at the École des Beaux-Arts in Aix-en-
Provence, France. Received further training at the
Chelsea School of Art, London. Lives and works
in Paris.

Selected Solo Exhibitions:
1986 *Art Aujourd'hui*, Lieu d'Artistes, Strasbourg,
    France
    Galerie Lola Gassin, Nice, France
1989 Musée de l'Institut du Monde Arabe, Paris
    Galerie Lola Gassin, Nice, France
    Galerie Keller, Paris
1991 Galerie Keller, Paris
1992 Galerie Becchie, Bastia, France

Selected Group Exhibitions:
1986 *Art Venir*, Espace Sextius, Aix-en-Provence,
    France
1987 Galerie Lola Gassin, Nice, France
    Galerie Monique Sarradet, Carcassonne,
    France
1988 Galerie Lola Gassin, Madrid, Spain
    Les Femmes dans les Arts Plastiques,
    Grand Palais, Paris
    Musée de Bastia, Bastia, France
1989 Palais des Congres, Marseilles, France
    Galerie Alain Oudin, Paris
    Foundation Vassarely, Aix-en-Provence,
    France
1990 Galerie Keller, Paris
    Jeune Peinture Niçoise, Tour du Treseau,
    Carcassonne, France
1991 Galerie Lola Gassin, Nice, France
1994 *Forces of Change: Artists of the Arab World*,
    The National Museum of Women in
    the Arts, Washington

Note: Information excerpted and edited from
Tahar Ben Jellon's and Jean-Luc Challumeau's
contribution to a Galerie Keller catalogue,
October-November 1989.

Huguette Caland
Born in Beirut, Lebanon, in 1931. Began painting
at age sixteen with the Italian artist Manetti in
Beirut. She studied art at the University of Beirut
from 1964 to 1968. In 1983 she began studying
sculpture with George Apostu.

Caland is a painter, sculptor, fashion designer and
filmmaker. She designed the *Nour* line for Pierre

Cardin which was presented at Espace Pierre
Cardin in 1979. She has been living and working
in Paris since 1970. Her work can be found in several museum collections in Paris.

Selected Solo Exhibitions:
1970 Dar-el-Fan, Beirut, Lebanon
1973 Galerie Contact, Beirut, Lebanon
1980 Galerie Faris, Paris
1992 Gallery 5, Santa Monica, Calif.
    Toepel Gallery, Kirkland, Wash.
1993 Bella Gallery, Santa Monica, Calif.

Selected Group Exhibitions:
1970 Traveling exhibition, Smithsonian
    Institution Traveling Exhibition Service
    (SITES), Washington
1971 *Contemporary Islamic Art*, Institute of
    Contemporary Art, London
1972 Contemporary Lebanese Artists, Museum
    of Art, Tokyo
    Grafica d'oggi, Venice Biennial, Venice, Italy
1973 *L'Estampe Contemporaine*, Bibliothèque
    Nationale, Paris
    International Festival of Painting, Cagnes-
    sur-Mer, Cagnes, France
1980 Arab Women Artists, Baghdad Museum
    of Art, Baghdad, Iraq
1984 Joan Miró Foundation, Barcelona, Spain
1985 Femina: In Memory of Alicia Penalba,
    UNESCO, Paris
    Le Mille et Une Nuits, Cultural Center of
    Bologne, Bologne, France
1986 Bibliothèque Nationale, Paris
    Monaco Art Center, Monte Carlo, Monaco
    Drawing '86, Pesci Gallery, Pécs, Hungary
1994 *Forces of Change: Artists of the Arab World*,
    The National Museum of Women in
    the Arts, Washington

Wasma'a K. Chorbachi
Born in Baghdad, Iraq, in 1944. Studied in Beirut,
Lebanon, and Florence, Italy. Earned Ph.D. in
the history of Islamic art from Harvard University
in Cambridge, Mass. She is a professor at both
Harvard and the Massachusetts Institute of
Technology in Cambridge.

Selected Solo Exhibitions:
1966 Beirut, Lebanon
1967 Florence, Italy
1968 Beirut, Lebanon
1970 Beirut, Lebanon
1976 Abū Dhabi, United Arab Emirates
1981 Jedda, Saudi Arabia
1983 Cambridge, Mass.
1984/
1985 London
1990 Al-Khubar, Saudi Arabia

Selected Group Exhibitions:
1964/
1970 Beirut, Lebanon
1967 Florence, Italy

1976/
1988 Cambridge, Mass.
1987 Washington
1981/
1990 Saudi Arabi
1984/
1989 London
1994 *Forces of Change: Artists of the Arab World,*
    The National Museum of Women in
    the Arts, Washington

Saloua Raouda Choucair

Born in Lebanon in 1916. Graduated from Beirut
College for Women in Lebanon in 1938. Studied
at the American University of Beirut and the
École Nationale des Beaux Arts in Paris during the
1940s and early 1950s. She received certificates
from both the Pratt Institute in New York and the
Cranbrook Academy of Art near Detroit in the
mid-1950s. Worked and exhibited in Paris from
1946 until 1952, learning much about the traditions of early 20th-century abstraction.

Choucair's 1947 exhibition at the Arab Cultural
Gallery in Beirut was the Arab world's first abstract painting exhibition. Her art is included in
the collections of numerous museums. One of
the Arab world's foremost sculptors, her work is
widely known and highly regarded. Now lives and
works in Beirut.

Selected Solo Exhibitions:
1947 Arab Cultural Gallery, Beirut, Lebanon
1951 Galerie Colette Alendy, Paris
1962 Matériels, UNESCO Center, Beirut, Lebanon
1974 Honorary retrospective, sponsored by the
    Lebanese Artists Association at the
    National Council of Tourism Showroom,
    Beirut, Lebanon
1977 Sculpture exhibition, Galerie Contact,
    Beirut, Lebanon
1988 Montada Gallery, Beirut (awarded Medal of
    Honor by the Prime Minister of Lebanon)
1993 Retrospective, Dar-al-Nadwah, Beirut,
    Lebanon (decorated as Honorary High
    Commander, Lebanese Government)

Selected Group Exhibitions:
1955/ Autumn Exhibition, Sursock Museum,
    Lebanon (yearly; awarded every annual
    prize until 1973)
1955/
1983 Spring Exhibition, Ministry of Education,
    Lebanon (yearly; awarded prize 1972)
1966 Musée Rodin, Paris
1968 Alexandria Biennial, Alexandria, Egypt
    (awarded 2nd prize)
1971 Salon des Réalités Nouvelles, Paris
1971/
1977 Salon de Mai, Paris (yearly)
1977 Salon des Réalitiés Nouvelles, Paris
1980 Women Artists, Baghdad, Iraq
1989/
1990 *Lebanon: The Artist's View,* London and Paris

1994 *Forces of Change: Artists of the Arab World,*
    The National Museum of Women in
    the Arts, Washington

Khulood Da'mi

Born in Baghdad, Iraq. Graduated from the
Academy of Arts in Baghdad. Studied ceramics
in London from 1987 to 1989. She is a member
of Iraqi Artists Association. A ceramist, designer
and cartoonist, Da'mi has taught in both London
and Algeria. Her work is in the collection of the
British Museum in London.

Solo Exhibition:
1991 Omphalos Gallery, London

Selected Group Exhibitions:
1988 *Arab Women Artists in the United Kingdom,*
    Kufa Gallery, London
1991 Four Gallery, London
1992 Kufa Gallery, London
1992 Black Art Gallery, London
    Tom Allen Art Center
    Greenwich Gallery
1994 *Forces of Change: Artists of the Arab World,*
    The National Museum of Women in
    the Arts, Washington

Inji Efflatoun

Born in Egypt in 1924; died in 1989. She received
her degree from Élevé au Sacré-Coeur and the
Lycée Français, and went on to study design and
painting with the Egyptian artist Kamel el-
Telmissany. She participated in exhibitions of the
Art and Freedom Group, one of the first organiza-
tions which attempted to free modern Egyptian
art from the bonds of academia and formalism.

In 1986 Efflatoun was awarded a medal of merit,
Cavalier of the Arts and Literature, from the
French Ministry of Culture. Her works have been
acquired by museums and private collectors
around the world. In addition to the exhibitions
listed below, she has had solo exhibitions in
Moscow, Cairo, Dresden, Warsaw, Prague and
New Dehli.

Selected Solo Exhibitions:
1952 Cairo, Egypt
1967 Galleria Nueva Pesa, Rome
    Galerie de l'Université, Paris
1981 Egyptian Academy, Rome, Italy
1985 Retrospective exhibition—1942–1985,
    Galerie Akhnaton, Cairo, Egypt

Selected Group Exhibitions:
1952 Venice Biennial, Venice, Italy
1953 São Paulo Biennial, São Paulo, Brazil
1968 Venice Biennial, Venice, Italy
1971 Contemporary Egyptian art exhibition, Paris
1989 *Retrospective en Hommage au Peintre Disparu,*
    Cairo Atelier, Cairo, Egypt
1992 *La Donna Egiziana e la Sua Creativita,*
    Egyptian Academy, Rome

1994 *Forces of Change: Artists of the Arab World*, The National Museum of Women in the Arts, Washington

Balqees Fakhro
Born in Bahrain in 1950. Received a bachelor of arts degree from Lone Mountain College in San Francisco, Calif., in 1975. She is a member of the Formative Art Society, as well as the Artists Group of the Arabian Gulf Cooperation Council.

Selected Group Exhibitions:
1977 Formative Art Society Exhibition, Bahrain
1984 Exhibition of Bahraini Female Artists, Bahrain
1985 National Day Exhibition of the Modern Art Society, Bahrain
      December Exhibition of the Formative Art Society, Bahrain
1986 Formative Art, Regional Conference for Women in the Gulf and Arabian Peninsula, Oman
      Artists Group of the Arabian Gulf Cooperation Council States, Kuwait City and Cairo (1986); Tunis and Madrid (1987); Amman and Bonn (1989); Washington (1990)
1988 Art for Humanity, Baghdad International Festival of Art, Baghdad, Iraq
1990 Art for Humanity, Baghdad International Festival of Art, Baghdad, Iraq
1994 *Forces of Change: Artists of the Arab World*, The National Museum of Women in the Arts, Washington

Rima Farah
Born in Amman, Jordan, in 1955. Received degrees from the Eastbourne School of Art in 1975 and Cambridge School of Art in 1978. She has collaborated closely with British artist Kevin Jackson since the early 1980s. One of her recent commissions was the design of greeting cards for UNICEF. Her work is in the collection of the Jordan National Museum of Fine Arts.

Selected Solo Exhibitions:
1984 Graffiti Gallery, London
1985 Arab Heritage Gallery, al-Khubar, Saudi Arabia
1986 Gallery Nuha Butchoen, Amman, Jordan
      Van Wagner Gallery, Ankara, Turkey
1987 Harrods Art Gallery, London
1989 Sultan Gallery, Kuwait City, Kuwait
1990 Majlis Gallery, Dubai, United Arab Emirates
1991 Rima and Kevin, Seibu Limited, Tokyo
      Tanger Flandria Art Gallery, Tangier, Morocco
1992 Alif Gallery, Cairo, Egypt
      Inma Gallery of Fine Art, Dhahran, Saudi Arabia

Selected Group Exhibitions:
1984 *Arab Artists*, Graffiti Gallery, London
1985 Islamic Cultural Center, London
1986 The Mall Gallery, London
      Falcon Gallery, Riyadh, Saudi Arabia
1989 Egee Art, London
1992 Alif Gallery, Washington
1994 *Forces of Change: Artists of the Arab World*, The National Museum of Women in the Arts, Washington

Maysaloon Faraj
Born in Hollywood, Calif., in 1955 to Iraqi parents. In 1967 she moved to Baghdad, Iraq, where she received her high school education. Earned a bachelor's degree in architecture from the University of Baghdad in 1989. Faraj continued her education between 1985 and 1991 at Fulham and Chelsea and at the Merton Institute.

Faraj has won numerous awards and received several commissions to execute wall panels and murals. For the past ten years she has divided her time between Baghdad, London and Paris, and she now resides in Surrey, England.

Selected Solo Exhibitions:
1985 Espace 2000, Paris
1987 River Gardens, London
1990 Rochan Gallery, London
      Argile Gallery, London

Selected Group Exhibitions:
1987 *Contemporary Arab Artists and Architects*, Islamic Cultural Center, London
1988 *Arab Women Artists in the United Kingdom*, Kufa Gallery, London
      Baghdad Biennial International Art Festival, Baghdad, Iraq
1990 National Gallery of Modern Art, Baghdad, Iraq
1991 Kufa Gallery, London
      Portobello Art Festival, Argile Gallery, London
1992 *Arab Women Artists*, Kufa Gallery, London
      Summer Exhibition, Howard Gallery, New Malden, Surrey, England
      Iraqi Women's Festival, Kufa Gallery, London
1994 *Forces of Change: Artists of the Arab World*, The National Museum of Women in the Arts, Washington

Fatima Hassan el-Farouj
Born in Tetouan, Morocco, in 1945. Has exhibited widely in the Arab world and to a substantial extent in Europe.

Selected Solo Exhibitions:
1966 Institut Goethe, Casablanca, Morocco
1969 Salle de Fêtes, Oujda, Morocco
1971 Centre Culturel Français, Rabat, Morocco
1973 Galerie Bab Rouah, Rabat, Morocco
1975 RFA, Bonn, Düsseldorf and Berlin, Germany

1976/
1979 Galerie Venise Cadre, Casablanca, Morocco
       (yearly)
1977 Institut Goethe, Casablanca, Morocco
1980 Musée Rade, Hamburg, Germany
1981 Galerie l'Atelier, Rabat, Morocco
       Galerie le Savouroux, Casablanca, Morocco
1982 Centre Culturel, Casablanca, Morocco

       Selected Group Exhibitions:
1965 Salon des Artistes Indépendants,
       Casablanca, Morocco
1966 *Panorama des Artistes Marocains*, Galerie Bab
       Rouah, Rabat, Morocco
       Exposition Internationale, Montreal, Canada
1969 Festival Panafricain, Algeria
1975 Exhibitions, Bonn, Berlin and Düsseldorf,
       Germany
1981 Salon d'Art Sacre, Paris
       Dix Ans a l'Atelier, Galerie Bab Rouah,
       Rabat, Morocco
       Huit Peintres du Monde Arabe, Assila
       Museum, Assila, Morocco
1985 *Peintres Naifs Marocains*, Ratha Museum,
       Fez, Morocco
1987 Traveling group exhibition, Brazil
1994 *Forces of Change: Artists of the Arab World*,
       The National Museum of Women in
       the Arts, Washington

Simone Fattal

Born in Damascus, Syria, in 1942. Studied philosophy at the École des Lettres in Beirut, Lebanon, and the Sorbonne in Paris. She is a painter and an art critic for Radio Lebanon. Illustrated Etel Adnan's book, *Five Senses for One Death* (Arabic edition, 1973).

In 1980 Fattal moved to the United States, where she founded a publishing house, the Post-Apollo Press, devoted to producing works by women. A versatile artist, she is the author of several short stories. She began work in photography in 1980 and sculpture in 1985.

       Selected Solo Exhibitions:
1973 Galerie One, Beirut, Lebanon
1992 Retrospective exhibition, Dar el-Nadwa,
       Beirut, Lebanon

       Selected Group Exhibitions:
1974 Dar el-Fan, Beirut, Lebanon
       Museum of Modern Art, Tokyo
1978 Espace Cardin, Paris
1979 Museum of Modern Art, Tunis, Tunisia
1983 Perception Gallery, San Francisco, Calif.
1984 Perception Gallery, San Francisco, Calif.
1994 *Forces of Change: Artists of the Arab World*,
       The National Museum of Women in
       the Arts, Washington

Amal Ftouni

Born in Beirut, Lebanon, in 1956. Resides in Melbourne, Australia. Received a post-graduate diploma in fine arts from the University of Lebanon in Beirut in 1983, and another in classical animation from Exeter College in England in 1988. Received a master's degree in electronic graphics from Coventry Polytechnic in England in 1989, and also holds a master's degree in American studies from the University of Exeter, England.

Ftouni was an art professor at Beirut University College in Lebanon from 1982 until 1985. She has produced several animated films and also produces computer animation. Her work can be found in several public collections.

       Selected Group Exhibitions:
1983 Carlton Hotel, Beirut, Lebanon
1984 Ministry of Tourism, Beirut, Lebanon
1985 Beit el-Dein Palace, Beirut, Lebanon
       Falougha Center, Falougha, Lebanon
1992 Arabic Festival, Melbourne, Australia
1994 *Forces of Change: Artists of the Arab World*,
       The National Museum of Women in
       the Arts, Washington

Lina Ghaibeh

Born in Damascus, Syria, in 1967. Resides in Beirut, Lebanon. Received a bachelor's degree in art from Beirut University College in 1988 and a master's degree in design with a minor in photography from Texas Women's University, Denton, Texas, in 1990. Her graduate thesis explored serious contemporary comics. Ghaibeh finds the atmosphere in her home city of Beirut open to creative discovery. She has recently been exploring computer graphics.

       Selected Group Exhibitions:
1986 Jadworkshop, Institut Goethe, Beirut and
       Tripoli, Lebanon
1988 First Festival of Comics, Beirut, Lebanon
       Jadworkshop, Beirut University College,
       Lebanon
       Galerie Saint Simone, France
1989 From Beirut, Dar el-Nadwa, Beirut,
       Lebanon
1990 Crée à Beyrouth, Comité de Jumelage,
       France
1991 Beirut: The Last Exit, Comité de Jumelage,
       France
1992 Institut Goethe, Beirut and Tripoli,
       Lebanon (first computer graphics exhibition in Lebanon)
1994 *Forces of Change: Artists of the Arab World*,
       The National Museum of Women in
       the Arts, Washington

Riham Ghassib

Born in Amman, Jordan. Works in a naive style from memory, using the Jordanian countryside and cultural ambiance as her subject matter. After high school in Jordan, Ghassib studied at Kansas State

University in Manhattan, Kansas. She has had two solo exhibitions in Amman and has been the subject of a television special. Her work can be found in several international private collections.

Samia Halaby
Born in Jerusalem in 1936. Left Palestine with the first wave of refugees in 1948. After three years in Beirut, her family moved to the United States. She received a bachelor's degree in design from the University of Cincinnati, Cincinnati, Ohio, in 1955. She continued her studies at Michigan State University in East Lansing, Mich., receiving a master's degree. Also secured a master of fine arts degree from Indiana University in 1963.

Halaby has taught art history and painting at the university level throughout the United States. She was a curator for the 22 Wooster Gallery in New York for a number of years. In 1982 she stopped teaching to devote her time to painting and writing. She has recently turned her talents to computer graphics. Her work can be found in numerous museum collections. She lives and works in New York.

Selected Solo Exhibitions:
1971   Phyllis Kind Gallery, Chicago, Ill.
1972   Yale School of Art Gallery, New Haven, Conn.
1973   The Spectrum Gallery, New York
1978   Marilyn Pearl Gallery, New York
1982   22 Wooster Gallery, New York
1983   Tossan-Tossan Gallery, New York
          Housatonic Museum, Bridgeport, Conn.
1986   Galería Palacio de Arte, Granada, Spain
1988   Tossan-Tossan Gallery, New York
1989   Gallery II, Michigan State University,
          East Lansing, Mich.
1993   911 Gallery, Indianapolis, Ind.

Selected Group Exhibitions:
1973   *American Drawing*, Yale Gallery,
          New Haven, Conn.
1974   The Wadsworth Atheneum, Hartford, Conn.
1975   *Recent Acquisitions*, Solomon R. Guggenheim
          Museum, New York
1977   Susan Caldwell Gallery, New York
          Contemporary American Printmaking, Indiana
          University Art Museum, Bloomington,
          Ind.
1979   *Arab Artists II*, Iraqi Cultural Center,
          London
1981   Palestinian Artists, Kunstnernes Hus, Oslo,
          Norway
1985   *Tamarind: 25 Years*, University Art Museum,
          Albuquerque, N. Mex.
1989   Havana Biennial, Museum of Fine Arts,
          Havana, Cuba
1990   Hilo International Exhibition, University
          of Hawaii, Hilo, Hawaii
1991   Sangre de Cristo Arts Center, Pueblo, Colo.
1994   *Forces of Change: Artists of the Arab World*,
          The National Museum of Women in
          the Arts, Washington

Tahia Halim
Born in Cairo, Egypt, in 1920. Studied in Cairo and Paris between 1941 and 1951. Has been a resident fellow in Egypt's Ministry of Arts and Culture since 1960. Halim has participated in forty-five exhibitions in Egypt, Europe and the United States. She has been awarded several medals for her art in Egypt. In 1958 she received a Guggenheim award. She is on the board of the Atelier for Artists and Writers, and in 1980 she became a board member of the Higher Council for the Arts. Her work is on display at the Museum of Modern Art, Cairo, Egypt; the Museum of Arts, Alexandria, Egypt; the Solomon R. Guggenheim Museum, New York; the National Museum, Warsaw, Poland; and Museum Antikli Corede in Italy.

Halim is a prolific ceramist. Her works were part of the exhibition *5000 Years of Egyptian Ceramics*, which toured European capitals in 1987. A composer as well as a visual artist, her "Quartet" has been performed at the Alexandria Atelier and broadcast on Radio Cairo. In 1990 her art was added to the collection of the Opera Museum in Cairo.

Selected Group Exhibitions:
n.d.   Venice Biennial, Venice, Italy
n.d.   Cairo Biennial, Cairo, Egypt
n.d.   Aladdin Hall, Cairo, Egypt
n.d.   Academy of the Arts, Alexandria, Egypt
n.d.   Numerau Hall, Florence, Italy
n.d.   Golden Circle, Zurich, Switzerland
n.d.   Paizi Nouvi, Rome
n.d.   Artigianoto, Rome
n.d.   Lornegria, Lausanne, Switzerland
n.d.   Institut Goethe, Cairo, Egypt
1994   *Forces of Change: Artists of the Arab World*,
          The National Museum of Women in
          the Arts, Washington

Mona Hatoum
Palestinian, born in Beirut in 1952. Studied at Beirut University College (1970–72), the Byam Shaw School of Art in London (1975–79) and the Slade School of Art in London (1979–81). Her interactive performances are meant to express the Palestinian experience during the past half century. Hatoum has been living and working in London since 1975.

Selected Solo Exhibitions:
1989   Galerie Oboro, Montreal, Canada
1992   *Dissected Space*, Chapter Art Centre,
          Cardiff, Wales
          Mario Fleche Gallery, London
1993   *Recent Work*, Arnolfini, Bristol, England
          Galerie Crousel-Robelin, Paris
1994   Galerie Rene Blouin, Montreal, Canada

Selected Group Exhibitions:
1988 *Edge 88*, International Festival of
    Experimental Art, London
1989 *Intimate Distance*, Photographers Gallery,
    London
    The Other Story, Hayward Gallery, London
1990 *Video and Myth*, Museum of Modern Art,
    New York
    British Art Show, McLellan Galleries, Leeds
    City Art Gallery and Hayward Gallery,
    England
1991 *Shocks to the System*, Royal Festival Hall,
    London
    Interrogating Identity, Grey Art Gallery,
    New York
    The Interrupted Life, New Museum of
    Contemporary Art, New York
1992 *Pour la Suite du Monde*, Musée d'Art
    Contemporain, Montreal
    *Manifeste: 30 ans de création en perspective,
    1960–1990*, Centre Georges Pompidou,
    Paris
1993 *Four Rooms*, Serpentine Gallery, London
    Positionings, Art Gallery of Ontario, Toronto,
    Canada
    Grazer Kombustion, Steirischer Herbst '93
    Festival, Graz, Austria
1994 *Forces of Change: Artists of the Arab World*,
    The National Museum of Women in
    the Arts, Washington

Fawzia el-Hicheri

Born in Nabeul, Tunisia, in 1946. Studied architecture, plastic and graphic arts, receiving a degree
from the Art Institute of Tunis in 1976. Graduated
from the Sorbonne in Paris in 1979 following studies in aesthetics and engraving.

El-Hicheri is an educator who is active in Tunisian
cultural affairs. She is a member of the Union
of Tunisian Artists and of a commission of the
Tunisian Ministry of Culture. Her work is in
several public collections in the Arab world.

Selected Solo Exhibitions:
1983 Ettaswir Gallery, Tunis, Tunisia
1991 Information Gallery, Tunis, Tunisia

Selected Group Exhibitions:
1983 First Biennial of Wood Engraving,
    Croissy-sur-Seine, France
1987 Plein Air, Bulgaria
    Cagnes-sur-Mer, Cagnes, France
1988 Ben Ghazi, Libya
    Galleria Rondanini, Rome
1989 Group Exhibition of Teachers at ITAAUT,
    Rabat, Morocco
1990 Assila Art Festival, Assila, Morocco
1992 National Festival of Tunisian Women,
    Hammamet, Tunisia
    Ajaccio Exhibition, Marseilles, France
1993 Tunisian Artists, Riyadh, Saudi Arabia
1994 *Forces of Change: Artists of the Arab World*,
    The National Museum of Women in
    the Arts, Washington

Nabila Hilmi

Palestinian born in Jerusalem in 1940. After
receiving two degrees in law, Hilmi received a
B.A. in fine arts from Beirut University College in
1983. Afterward she studied at the Art Students
League in New York. She also took courses in art
theory at the Barnes Foundation in Pennsylvania.

Selected Solo Exhibitions:
1978 Banouche Art Gallery, Bahrain
1988 Addison/Ripley Gallery, Washington
1989 Cherif Fine Art Gallery, Tunis, Tunisia

Selected Group Exhibitions:
1987 Baltimore Museum of Art, Baltimore, Md.
1988 Abdul Hameed Shoman Foundation,
    Amman, Jordan
    Baltimore Museum of Art, Baltimore, Md.
1989 Royal Cultural Center, Amman, Jordan
1990 From Realism to Abstraction, Abdul
    Hameed Shoman Foundation, Amman,
    Jordan
1991 *People*, Capitol Hill Art League, Washington
    Alif Gallery, Washington
    Galleria Civica d'Arte Contemporanea,
    Marsala, Italy
    Abdul Hameed Shoman Foundation,
    Amman, Jordan
    Works on Paper, Capitol Hill Art League,
    Washington
1992 *12 × 12*, Foundry Gallery, Washington
    New Directions, Capitol Hill Art League,
    Washington
    Intimate Interiors, Capitol Hill Art League,
    Washington
    A Dialogue in Expression, Jordan National
    Gallery of Fine Arts, Amman, Jordan
1993 *The Blues*, Capitol Hill Art League,
    Washington
1994 *Forces of Change: Artists of the Arab World*,
    The National Museum of Women in
    the Arts, Washington

Jumana el-Husseini

Born in Jerusalem in 1932. Left Jerusalem for
Beirut in 1948 and presently resides in Paris.
Studied painting, ceramics and sculpture while
majoring in political science at the American
University of Beirut and the Beirut College for
Women during the 1950s. El-Husseini is a painter
and sculptor who has won many medals and has
an extensive international exhibition record.

Selected Solo Exhibitions:
1965 Woodstock Gallery, London
1968 German Cultural Center, Beirut, Lebanon
    German Cultural Center, Tripoli, Lebanon
1970 American University of Beirut,
    Beirut, Lebanon
1971 Bonn University, Bonn, Germany
    Stuttgart University, Stuttgart, Germany
    Staedtische Galerie Imlanbachhaus,
    Munich, Germany
1973 Galleria Delta, Rome
    Galerie Antiquaire, Beirut, Lebanon

1979 Jedda Dome, Jedda, Saudi Arabia
1981 Redec Gallery, Jedda, Saudi Arabia
1984 Arab Heritage Gallery, Dahran, Saudi Arabia
1987 Tour of United States and Canada sponsored by the Palestine Human Rights Campaign
1989 Soviet Friendship Center, Moscow
Addison/Ripley Gallery, Washington
Georgetown University, Washington
1990 Galerie Étienne Dinet, Paris
Argile Gallery, London
Shoman Gallery, Amman, Jordan
1993 Gallery Anadiel, Jerusalem

Selected Group Exhibitions:
1960 Sursok Museum, Beirut, Lebanon
1966 Centre Culturel, Paris
Centre Culturel, Brussels
1969 Exhibition of Contemporary Artists, London
Alexandria Biennial, Alexandria, Egypt
1970 Symposium on Palestine, Kuwait City, Kuwait
1971 Arab Artists Exhibition, Damascus, Syria
1971/
1973 Traveling exhibition, Smithsonian Institution Traveling Exhibition Service (SITES), Washington
1972 Delta Gallery, Beirut, Lebanon
Galleria Labercatia, Rome
1973 Tenth International Youth Festival, Berlin
Kuwait Biennial, Kuwait City, Kuwait
1974 Baghdad Biennial, Baghdad, Iraq
Arab Artists Exhibition, Beirut, Lebanon
1975 Union of Arab Artists Exhibition, traveling to Algeria, Morocco and Tunisia
1978 Japanese Society for Afro-Asian Artists, Tokyo
1979 Venice Biennial, Venice, Italy
Beaux Arts of Lisbon, Lisbon, Portugal
United Nations, Geneva, Switzerland
1980 Museum of Oriental Art, Moscow
National Museum, Madrid, Spain
Museum of Ceramics, Zaragoza, Spain
Museum of Modern Art, Warsaw, Poland
Ausstellungs Zentum, Frensektum, Berlin
House of Culture, Eitensheim, Germany
Cultural Center, Bytów, Poland
1981 Kunstnernes Hus, Oslo, Norway
Cultural Center, Armenia
1982 Christiansands Kunts Forening, Norway
Arab University of Beirut, Beirut, Lebanon
UNESCO, Paris
1983 The Friends House, London
1984 Concert House, Stockholm
1985 Palais des Congres et de la Culture d'Orient, Paris
Mall Gallery, London
1986 Centre des Unions Cretiennes, Geneva, Switzerland
Traveling exhibition, Tokyo
Arab League, Paris
Salle d'Exposition de Sépulcre, Caen, France
Hall d'Honneur d'Exposition Hôtel de

Ville, Brest, France
Pavillon le Verdurier, Limoges, France
Salle des Expositions Hôtel de Ville, Carcassonne, France
Galeries du Vestibule de la Salle Aragon, Hôtel de Ville, Perpignan, France
Galeries Passerelle et Mathurnin, Tours, France
1987 Kuwait Group Exhibition sponsored by the Union of Palestinian Women, Kuwait City, Kuwait
1988 Messe Palace, Vienna
Museum of Modern Art, Tokyo
1989 Barbican Centre, London
Musée de l'Institut du Monde Arabe, Paris
1990 Hôtel de Ville, Douai, France
1991 Espace Voltaire, Paris
1992 Grand Palais, Paris
1993 Réalités Nouvelles, Grand Palais, Paris
Shoman Gallery, Amman
1994 *Forces of Change: Artists of the Arab World*, The National Museum of Women in the Arts, Washington

Kamala Ishaq Ibrahim
Born in Sudan. Trained at the Faculty of Fine Arts in Khartoum, Sudan, and continued her art studies at the Royal College in London. Ibrahim's works are distinctive for their expressionistic distortion.

Siham Abu Acle Jaar
Born in Bethlehem in 1937. She received a certificate from St. Joseph de l'Apparition in Bethlehem in 1951. A self-taught artist, she received no formal training. Jaar first showed her work in a city-sponsored exhibition in Paris, and has participated annually in this show held at the Grand Palais. She uses painting to express her feelings in a personal way. She currently resides in Paris. Her art is included in *Forces of Change: Artists of the Arab World*, at The National Museum of Women in the Arts, Washington (1994).

Ghada Jamal
Born in Beirut in 1955. Received a bachelor's degree in art from Beirut University College in 1984 and a master's degree in fine arts from California State University, Long Beach, in 1991.

For the past ten years Jamal has divided her time between California, England and Lebanon. The subject matter of her art is the war-torn landscape of Lebanon, to which she feels emotionally tied. She has received several awards for her art. Her work is in a number of private collections internationally. She currently resides in Anaheim, California.

Selected Solo Exhibitions:
1985 Mystic Expressions, Beirut University College, Beirut, Lebanon
1990 *Lebanese Landscapes*, California State Univeristy, Long Beach, Calif.

Selected Group Exhibitions:

1986 Autumn Salon, Sursock Museum, Beirut, Lebanon

Beit al-Dein Annual, Beit al-Dein Palace, Lebanon

1988 Alumni Exhibition, Beirut University College, Beirut, Lebanon

1989 *Group '89*, California State University, Long Beach, Calif.

1990 Long Beach Art Expedition, Printworks Gallery, Long Beach, Calif.

WAM, Downey Museum of Art, California

Group 390, California State University, Long Beach, Calif.

1991 Angel's Gate Cultural Center Members Exhibition, San Pedro, Calif.

1992 World News, Muckenthaler Cultural Center, Fullerton, Calif.

Beyond Baroque, Venice, Calif.

The Onyx, Los Angeles, Calif.

LA Abstract Artists: Works on Paper, Gallery X, Exeter, England

1993 Four Arab Artists from the United States, Abdul Hameed Shoman Foundation, Amman, Jordan

1994 *Forces of Change: Artists of the Arab World*, The National Museum of Women in the Arts, Washington

Liliane Karnouk

Born in Cairo, Egypt, in 1944. Received a degree from the Academy of Fine Arts in Rome in 1966. She did postgraduate work in communications at Concordia University in Montreal and received a master's degree in art education from the University of British Columbia in Vancouver in 1982. Karnouk has been the recipient of several grants and awards, among them a Ford Foundation grant for 1982 through 1985. Her work is in several museum collections. She resides in Vancouver, Canada.

Selected Solo Exhibitions:

1982 Desertscapes, Goethe Institute, Alexandria, Egypt

Desertscapes, National Art Center, Cairo, Egypt

1985 Miniatures & Books, Goethe Institute, Cairo, Egypt

Miniatures & Books, Ostracca Gallery, Alexandria, Egypt

Sabra & Shatilla, Goethe Institute, Cairo, Egypt

1987 Paper Flying Carpets, Italian Cultural Center, Cairo, Egypt

1988 Hautungen, Galerie IFA, Bonn, Germany

1992 Ibrahim, Centre d'Exposition de la Gare, Quebec City, Canada

Black & Green, Goethe Institute, Cairo, Egypt

Eastern Desert, Galerie La Part du Sable, Cairo, Egypt

Selected Group Exhibitions:

1983 Desertscapes, Samia Zeitun Gallery, Cairo, Egypt

Alexandria Biennial, Museum of Modern Art, Alexandria, Egypt

1986 International Biennial of Paper Art, Leopold-Hoesch Museum, Düren, Germany

1990 Acht Kunstler Aus Agypten, Galerie der Kongresshalle, Augsburg, Germany

Aesthetica Diffusa 4, Salerno, Italy

1991 Papier Parallel, Neuer Kunstverein, Aschaffenburg, Germany

Acht Kunstler Aus Agypten, Rosenheim, Germany

ECART, Boreal Multimedia, Centre d'Exposition de la Gare, L'Annonciation, Quebec City, Canada

ECART, Boreal Multimedia, KIO Kunstnersenteret, Lillehammer, Norway

Natura Mater, Centro Internazionale Multimedia, Sint-Baafs-Vigve, Belgium

Storia Naturale, Museum of Genoa, Genoa, Italy

1994 *Forces of Change: Artists of the Arab World*, The National Museum of Women in the Arts, Washington

Leila Kawash

Born in Baghdad, Iraq, in 1945. Received a degree in design from the Manchester College of Art in 1966. Her recent work is characterized by an interest in Arabic calligraphy. She is one of Iraq's most distinguished artists.

Selected Solo Exhibitions:

1978 Hilton Hotel, Abū Dhabi, United Arab Emirates

1982 Sheraton Hotel, Abū Dhabi, United Arab Emirates

1984/
1986 *Through Arab Eyes* (traveling exhibition), Milwaukee Library, University of Wisconsin-Milwaukee, Wis.; Cupples House Art Gallery, St. Louis University, Saint Louis, Mo.; The Kennedy Center, Brigham Young University; Provo, Utah; Birmingham Public Library, Atlanta, Ga.

1985 Hilton Hotel, Athens, Greece

Selected Group Exhibitions:

1989 Alif Gallery, Washington

1990 Braathen Nusseibah Gallery, New York

1991 Alif Gallery, Washington

1994 *Forces of Change: Artists of the Arab World*, The National Museum of Women in the Arts, Washington

Helen Khal

Born in Allentown, Pa., in 1932 of Lebanese parents. Studied at the Lebanese Academy of Fine Arts in Beirut from 1946 to 1948 and at the Art Students League, New York, in 1948 and 1949.

Khal is not only a painter but also an educator, critic, public lecturer and author. She has won many awards, including the Medal of Honor at the Alexandria Biennial in 1968. Khal also is well known for her book *The Woman Artist in Lebanon* (1987). She currently lives and works in Washington.

Selected Solo Exhibitions:
1960 Galerie Alecco Saab, Beirut, Lebanon
1966 Galerie Feuille d'Or, Beirut, Lebanon
1968 Galerie Manoug, Beirut, Lebanon
1969 First National Bank, Allentown, Pa.
1970 Studio Caland, Kaslik, Lebanon
1972 Contact Art Gallery, Beirut, Lebanon
1974 Contact Art Gallery, Beirut, Lebanon
1975 Bolivar Gallery, Kingston, Jamaica
     Contact Art Gallery, Beirut, Lebanon
1983 Georgetown Design Group, Washington
1988 Maksoud Residence, Washington
1991 Alwan Gallery, Kaslik, Lebanon

Selected Group Exhibitions:
1963/
1993 Autumn Salon, Sursock Museum, Beirut, Lebanon (yearly)
1965/
1993 Spring Salon, Ministry of Education, Beirut, Lebanon (yearly)
1967 São Paulo Biennial, São Paulo, Brazil
1969 Alexandria Biennial, Alexandria, Egypt
1971 Art of Lebanon, Tokyo, Japan
     Alexandria Biennial, Alexandria, Egypt
1973 Alexandria Biennial, Alexandria, Egypt
1975 Kings College, Wilkes Barre, Pa.
1980 Galerie Faris, Paris
     Arab Artists, Alif Gallery, Washington
1985 *Arab Artists*, Alif Gallery, Washington
1986 Baghdad International Festival of Art, Saddam Center, Baghdad, Iraq
1988 *Arab Artists*, Alif Gallery, Washington
1993 Shoman Gallery, Amman, Jordan
1994 *Forces of Change: Artists of the Arab World*, The National Museum of Women in the Arts, Washington

Sabiha Khemir
Born in Tunisia in 1959. Graduated from the University of Tunis with a B.A. in English literature in 1983. Received her M.A. (1986) and Ph.D. (1990) from London University, School of Oriental and African Studies. Teaches in England and the United States, and has lectured extensively on Islamic art throughout Europe.

Khemir authored *Waiting in the Future for the Past to Come* (1993) and contributed essays to the catalogue *Al-Andalus: Islamic Arts of Spain* (1992) for the Metropolitan Museum of Art. She has illustrated books and designed book covers. She also has been active in cinema and television in France and England. Her works are in private collections in England.

Selected Group Exhibitions:
1980 Centre National d'Art et de Culture Georges Pompidou (Beaubourg), Paris
1986 The Islamic Centre, London
1987 *The Book Cover*, Kufa Gallery, London
1988 *Arab Women Artists in the United Kingdom*, Kufa Gallery, London
1993 Kufa Gallery, London
1994 *Forces of Change: Artists of the Arab World*, The National Museum of Women in the Arts, Washington

Nazli Madkour
Born in Cairo, Egypt, in 1949. Studied economics and political science at Cairo University. She received a diploma in management and a master's degree in political economy from the American University in Cairo.

After 1981 Madkour turned her attention to the arts, studying informally in Egypt and Italy. She has participated extensively in group shows in Egypt and abroad. She is a member of the Syndicate of Plastic Arts, the Friends of Art and the Cairo Atelier. She published *Women and Art in Egypt* (1989). Her work is in the collections of several museums throughout the Arab world.

Selected Solo Exhibitions:
1982 The American Cultural Center, Cairo, Egypt
     Morgan State University, Baltimore, Md.
1983 Akhnaton Gallery, Cairo, Egypt
1984 Town Hall of the City of Ottowa, Ottowa, Canada
     Akhnaton Gallery, Cairo, Egypt
1985 The Egyptian Cultural Center, Paris
1986 Akhnaton Gallery, Cairo, Egypt
1987 Arts and Crafts Gallery, Amsterdam, Holland
1988 Akhnaton Gallery, Cairo, Egypt
1990 Akhnaton Gallery, Cairo, Egypt
1991 Alexandria Atelier, Alexandria, Egypt
1992 Akhnaton Gallery, Cairo, Egypt
1994 *Forces of Change: Artists of the Arab World*, The National Museum of Women in the Arts, Washington

Baya Mahieddine
Born in Algeria in 1931. Baya is a completely self-taught artist. She was adopted at the age of five by a French couple living in Algeria. She never learned to read and write. At the age of sixteen she had an exhibition in France which brought her to the attention of André Breton and Pablo Picasso. Her preferred medium is gouache on paper. She has rarely exhibited outside of France and her native land. She lives in Blida, Algeria, where she continues to paint actively.

Selected Solo Exhibitions:
1947 Galerie Adrien Maeght, Paris
1966 Galerie Pilote, Algiers, Algeria
1969 Centre Culturel Français, Algiers, Algeria

1976 Centre Culturel Français, Algiers, Algeria
1977 Maison de la Culture, Tizi Ouzou, Algeria
1978 Galerie Muḥammad Racim, Algiers, Algeria
1980 Centre Culturel Français, Algiers, Algeria
1982 Musée Cantini, Marseilles, France
1984 Centre Culturel Algérien, Paris

Selected Group Exhibitions:
1963 Salle Ibn Khaldoun, Algiers, Algeria
1964 Musée des Arts Decoratifs, Paris
1964 Galerie 54, Algiers, Algeria
1967 Galerie de l'Union Nationale des Arts
        Plastiques, Algiers, Algeria
1969 Galerie de l'UNAP, Algiers, Algeria
1971 Galerie de l'UNAP, Algiers, Algeria
1973 Galerie des 4 Colonnes, Algiers, Algeria
1974 Galerie Muḥammad Racim, Algiers, Algeria
1978 Galerie Muḥammad Racim, Algiers, Algeria
1984 Centre Culturel Communal, Aubagne,
        France
1987 Galerie Muhammad Issiakhem, Algiers,
        Algeria
1988 *Bonjour Picasso*, Musée Picasso, Antibes,
        France
1990 Musée de l'Institut du Monde Arabe, Paris
1994 *Forces of Change: Artists of the Arab World*,
        The National Museum of Women in
        the Arts, Washington

Nadira Mahmoud

Born in Oman in 1959. Studied law and pursued a career in the Ministry of Civil Service. She has been awarded various medals and certificates of distinction from countries in the region. Her works are included in several regional collections.

Selected Solo Exhibitions:
1989 Emirates Arts Association, Sharja, Oman
1991 Ashtar Auditorium, Damascus, Syria
1992 The Cultural Club, Quern, Oman

Selected Group Exhibitions:
1989 Arab Artists Exhibition, Kuwait City,
        Kuwait
        British-Oman Friendship Week,
        The Cultural Club, Oman
1990 Emirates Arts Association, Oman
1990 Sultan Qaboos Sports Complex, Oman
1991 National Day Celebration, Oman
1992 Doha Sheraton Exhibition Hall, Qatar
1994 *Forces of Change: Artists of the Arab World*,
        The National Museum of Women in
        the Arts, Washington

Seta Manoukian

Born in Beirut, Lebanon, in 1945 to Armenian parents. Studied at the Barking College of Technology in London. In 1966 she received a master's degree from the Academy of Fine Arts in Rome. She is the author of *Lebanese Children and the War* (1976). Manoukian, who has had a distinguished career, is the recipient of several awards and substantial media coverage. Her work can be found in many international corporate and private collections.

Selected Solo Exhibitions:
1967 Galerie Alecco Saab, Beirut, Lebanon
1971 Institut Goethe, Beirut, Lebanon
1979 Galerie Rencontre, Beirut, Lebanon
1984 Galerie Elissar, Beirut, Lebanon
1987 Armenian Cultural Center, Los Angeles,
        Calif.
1990 *Balancing Imbalances*, Gallery Casa Sin
        Nombre, Santa Fe, N. Mex.
1991 *Fractured Dialogues*, Alif Gallery, Washington
1992 *The Practical Use of Desire*, Sherry Frumkin
        Gallery, Santa Monica, Calif.

Selected Group Exhibitions:
1966 Fine Arts Academy of Rome, Rome
1967/
1975 Annual Spring Exhibition, UNESCO, Beirut,
        Lebanon
1972 Galerie Contact, Beirut, Lebanon
        Contemporary Lebanese Painters, Brigitte
        Shahade Gallery (traveling exhibition
        touring major cities in Germany)
        Wasiti Festival, Modern Art Museum,
        Baghdad, Iraq
        Grenier des Artistes, 2è Salon de Peintres
        Temoins de Leur Pays, Beirut, Lebanon
1974 Galerie Contemporain, Beirut, Lebanon
1981 Sursock Museum, Beirut, Lebanon
1984 Journalists Union Hall, Yerevan, Armenia
1985 Galerie Elissar, Beirut, Lebanon
        Cent Ans d'Art Plastique au Liban, Richard
        Shahene Gallery (traveling exhibition
        touring major cities in Brazil)
1989 The Artist's View: Two Hundred Years of
        Lebanese Painting, Musée de l'Institut
        du Monde Arabe, Paris
1989 Ricco Gallery, Los Angeles, Calif.
1991 *Contemporary Portraits*, Art Space Gallery,
        Los Angeles, Calif
        Two from Beirut, Sherry Frumkin Gallery,
        Santa Monica, Calif.
1994 *Forces of Change: Artists of the Arab World*,
        The National Museum of Women in
        the Arts, Washington

Rima Mardam-Bey

Born in Syria in 1948. Received her high school education in Damascus, Syria, and graduated from Beirut Protestant College in Lebanon. Studied art privately in Bern, Switzerland, and in Paris. Attended Heatherley School of Art in London during 1991 and 1992.

Selected Solo Exhibitions:
1975 Al-Nahda Women's Club, Riyadh,
        Saudi Arabia
1981 Patrick Seale Gallery, London

Selected Group Exhibitions:
1976 The American Arts and Crafts Club, Riyadh,
        Saudi Arabia
1986 Riayat al-Shabab, Riyadh, Saudi Arabia
1994 *Forces of Change: Artists of the Arab World*,
        The National Museum of Women in
        the Arts, Washington

Mounirah Mosly

Born in Mecca, Saudi Arabia, in 1952. She graduated from the College of Fine Arts in Cairo, Egypt, in 1972, and earned a degree in graphic arts in California in 1978. Mosly is a painter, teacher and graphic designer. An art critic, she contributes regularly to Saudi newspapers. Her work is in several corporate and museum collections, including the Museum of Modern Art in Madrid.

Selected Group Exhibitions:
1972 Ash-Shams Gallery, Jeddah, Saudi Arabia
1984 Dhahran Arts Goup, Dhahran, Saudi Arabia
1985 Arts and Culture Society, Damman, Saudi Arabia
1985/
1988 Exhibitions of the Gulf Cooperation Council (GCC),
 United Arab Emirates, Bahrain, Qatar, Saudi Arabia, Kuwait, Egypt, Tunisia and Spain
1986 Art for Humanity, Baghdad, Iraq
1988 Gulf Art Friends Exhibition, Jordan National Museum of Fine Arts, Amman, Jordan
1989 Gulf Art Friends Exhibition, Museum of Modern Art, Santo Domingo, Dominican Republic
 First Periodical Exhibition of Plastic Arts in the GCC States, Riyadh, Saudi Arabia
1991 *International Exhibition: Art from Arab and Islamic Countries*, Barbican Centre, London (traveled to several European capitals)
1994 *Forces of Change: Artists of the Arab World*, The National Museum of Women in the Arts, Washington

Layla Muraywid

Born in Damascus, Syria, in 1956. Educated at the École de Beaux-Arts de Dames in Damascus, and the École Nationale Supérieure des Arts Decoratifs in Paris. Muraywid has lived and worked in Paris since 1981. Her work is included in various European public and private collections.

Selected Solo Exhibitions:
1989 Cité Internationale des Arts, Paris
1990 Credit Lyonnais, Paris
1991 Galerie Marquet de Vasselot, Paris
1992 *Decouvertes*, Grand Palais, Paris
 Galerie Marlie Hanstein, Sarrebruck, Paris
1993 Galerie 50 × 70, Beirut, Lebanon

Selected Group Exhibitions:
1983 Maison de la Poesie, Paris
1984 International Miniprint, Cadaques, Paris
1986 Salon des Réalités Nouvelles, Grand Palais, Paris
1987 C.R.A.C., Champigny-sur-Marne, Paris
1988 Chelsea Old Town Hall, London
1990 Salon de Montrouge, Paris
 Cité Internationale des Arts, Paris
 Galerie La Teinturerie, Paris
 Galerie La Nouvelle Garvure, Paris

1991 20 Ans, 10 Artistes, Galerie L'Atelier, Rabat, Morocco
 Galerie Marlie Hanstien, Sarrebruck, Paris
1992 Biennale d'Art Contemporain, Drancy, Paris
 Galerie Marquet de Vasselot, Paris
 Galerie Marlies Hanstein, Sarrebruck, Paris
1993 Galerie Akie Aricchi, Paris
1994 *Forces of Change: Artists of the Arab World*, The National Museum of Women in the Arts, Washington

Effat Nagui

Born in Alexandria, Egypt, in 1912. Studied painting with her brother, Mohammad Nagy, and was a student of the French artist and critic André Lhote. After studying drawing, literature and music under her brother's tutelage from 1947 to 1950, Nagui joined the Egyptian Academy of Fine Arts in Rome. She later studied folk art with her husband, artist Saad el-Khadem.

Nagui's writings and drawings were published in France, and her musical studies and quartets have been performed in Egypt. She has received several National Creativity Grants from the Egypt's Ministry of Culture, and has also been awarded a number of medals and certificates of merit for her work.

Selected Solo Exhibitions:
n.d. Alexandria Atelier, Alexandria, Egypt
n.d. Alaa al-Din Gallery, Cairo, Egypt
n.d. Art for All Gallery, Cairo, Egypt
n.d. Fine Arts Museum, Alexandria, Egypt
n.d. French Cultural Center, Alexandria, Egypt
n.d. Hilton Gallery, Cairo, Egypt
n.d. Akhknaton Gallery, Cairo, Egypt
n.d. Galleria Numiro, Florence, Italy
n.d. Golden Circle Gallery, Zurich, Switzerland
n.d. Galleria Paese Nove, Rome
n.d. Gallerie Artigiano, Rome
n.d. Galerie l'Orangerie, Lausanne, Switzerland
n.d. Galleria Municipal, Antiche Corado, Italy
n.d. Palace of Culture, Alexandria, Egypt
1992 Effat Nagui: Fifty Years of Creativity, al-Kandeel Gallery, Alexandria, Egypt

Selected Group Exhibitions:
n.d. Venice Biennial, Venice, Italy
n.d. Alexandria Governors Exhibition of Twenty Artists, Paris, Madrid and Barcelona, Spain
1994 *Forces of Change: Artists of the Arab World*, The National Museum of Women in the Arts, Washington

Marguerite Nakhle

Born 1908 in Alexandria, Egypt; died in 1977. A Pioneer Artist and the leading realist of Egypt, Nakhle created such vivid works as *al-Suq* (Market) and *Horse Race*. She studied in Paris between 1934 and 1939, winning the annual student's medals at the Academy of the Arts in Paris from 1936 to 1938. She returned to Paris in the 1950s for further study.

In 1967 Nakhle was commissioned by the Coptic Church to produce twelve religious scenes about Christ, which she executed in the Coptic style. She also created *The Last Supper* and *The Birth of Christ* for the Coptic Church in Zamâlik, Cairo, Egypt.

Selected Solo Exhibitions:
1936 Aniyir, France
1948 Egyptian Embassy, Paris

Selected Group Exhibitions:
1949 Egypt-France Exhibition, Ceramic Art Museum
1954 Bernham, France
1958 International Cairo Exhibit, Cairo, Egypt
1959 Cairo Salon Exhibition, Cairo, Egypt
1960 Duville, France
1965 Cairo, Egypt
1994 *Forces of Change: Artists of the Arab World*, The National Museum of Women in the Arts, Washington

Hind Nasser

Born in Amman, Jordan. Received a bachelor's degree in political science and history from Beirut Women's College in Lebanon in 1961. Nasser studied art at the Fahrelnissa Zeid Royal Institute of Fine Arts in Amman from 1976 unit 1981. A cultural activist, she is intent on increasing public awareness of the value of art. She is an abstract painter who has received substantial critical attention.

Selected Solo Exhibitions:
1982 Alia Gallery, Amman, Jordan
1983 Association of Jordanian Artists, Amman, Jordan
1984 Royal Cultural Center, Amman, Jordan
1986 Marriott Hotel, Amman, Jordan
      Petra Bank Gallery, Amman, Jordan
1988 Tempera Art Gallery, London
1989 The Intercontinental, Abu Dhabi, United Arab Emirates
1992 Royal Cultural Center, Amman, Jordan

Selected Group Exhibitions:
1981 Fahrelnissa Zeid Royal Institute of Fine Arts, Palace of Culture, Amman, Jordan
     Spring Festival of the Jordanian Artists Association, Amman and Aqala, Jordan
     Salon d'Automne, Grand Palais, Paris
1982 Jordanian Cultural Week, Moscow
1983 Arab Women's Creative Art, Amman, Jordan
     Jerash Festival Exhibition, Jordan
     Prix du Peinture Ida Wingerter, Fenetrange, France
     Prix du Peinture et Sculpture, Strasbourg, France
     Salon d'Automne, Grand Palais, Paris
1984 Jordanian Artists Association, Royal Cultural Center, Amman, Jordan
     Jordanian Painters Exhibition, Amman, Jordan
     Salon d'Automne, Grand Palais, Paris

Jerash Festival Exhibition, Jordan
1985 Jordanian Painters Exhibition, Amman, Jordan
1987 Jordanian Painters Exhibition, Amman, Jordan
     British Graduates Exhibition, Amman, Jordan
1988 Jordanian Artists Association Exhibition, Amman, Jordan
1994 *Forces of Change: Artists of the Arab World*, The National Museum of Women in the Arts, Washington

Rabab Nemr

An Egyptian artist, Nemr graduated from the Faculty of Fine Arts in Alexandria in 1963 and later earned a doctorate in art from the San Fernando Academy, University of Madrid, in 1977. She is a member of the Syndicate of Fine Artists, the Cairo Atelier and the Alexandria Atelier. She has been department Director for the Plastic Arts at the Palaces of Culture in Alexandria. She has participated in numerous group exhibitions in Egypt and abroad (Jordan, Bulgaria, Kuwait, India, Qatar and Rumania), along with yearly national exhibitions held in Cairo and Alexandria.

Among the collections in which Nemr's work appears are the Tito Museum in Yugoslavia, the Egyptian Culture Center in Paris, the Museum of Modern Art in Jordan and the International Conference Center in Cairo. She currrently lives and works in Rome.

Selected Solo Exhibitions:
1984 Akhnaton Gallery, Cairo, Egypt
     Ragab Papyrus Gallery, Cairo, Egypt
     Palace of Culture Gallery, Alexandria, Egypt
     Muhammad Nagy Gallery, Alexandria, Egypt
1985 Seif Wanly Gallery, Alexandria, Egypt
1986 Akhnaton Gallery, Cairo, Egypt
     Ragab Papyrus Gallery, Cairo, Egypt
     Seif Wanly Gallery, Alexandria, Egypt
     Palace of Culture Gallery, al-Arish, Egypt
1987 Abyia Gallery, Kuwait City, Kuwait
1988 Akhnaton Gallery, Cairo, Egypt

Selected Group Exhibitions:
1994 *Forces of Change: Artists of the Arab World*, The National Museum of Women in the Arts, Washington

Houria Niati

Born in Khemis-Miliana, Algeria, in 1948. She received a diploma in community work, which included studies in visual art and music, from the National School of Tixeraine in Algeria in 1969. She studied drawing at the Camden Art Center and received a degree in fine arts from Croydon College of Art. A painter, singer and poet, Niati often accompanies her painting exhibitions with Algerian songs from a classical Andalusian repertoire and reads her own poetry written in French. Her work has received critical attention.

Selected Solo Exhibitions:
1984 *Delirium*, Africa Center, London
Echoes, The Art Show Gallery, London
Repercussions, Maison de la Culture,
Tizi Ouzou, Algeria
1985 Two-Artist Show (with her father, Khelifa
Niati) Annual Cultural Festival, Khemis-
Miliana, Algeria
Coming Back Show, Art Show Gallery,
London
One-Day Show, Smith's Gallery, London
1987 Maison de la Culture, Courbevoie, France
1988/
1989 *Mystery and Metaphor*, Ikon Gallery,
Birmingham, England
(traveling exhibition)
1990 Rochan Gallery, London
Small Mansion Art Center, London

Selected Group Exhibitions:
1984 *Into the Open*, Mappin Art Gallery, Sheffield,
Nottingham and Newcastle, England
1985 International Art Fair, Olympia, London
Open Exhibition, Riverside Studio, London
1986 *Third World Within*, Brixton Art Gallery and
Whitechapel Galleries, London
1987 Quatre Peintres au Féminin, Galerie
Issiakhem, Algeria
1988 Kufa Gallery, London
Central Space, London
1989 *Forums of Intuition*, Cartwright Hall
Museum, Bradford, England
Contemporary Art from the Islamic World,
Barbican Centre, London
1991 *Four by 4*, Harris Museum, Preston, England
1994 *Forces of Change: Artists of the Arab World*,
The National Museum of Women in
the Arts, Washington

Maisoon Saqr al-Qasimi

Poet and artist Maisoon Saqr al-Qasimi was born
in Abū Dhabi, the United Arab Emirates in 1958.
She received a master's in economics and political
science from the University of Cairo in 1981.

Selected Solo Exhibitions:
1990 Cultural Foundation Exhibition Center,
Abū Dhabi, U.A.E.
Alatelia Alopera, Cairo, Egypt
1991 Cultural Foundation Exhibition Center,
Abū Dhabi, U.A.E.
Alatelia Alopera, Cairo, Egypt
1993 Cultural Foundation Exhibition Center,
Abū Dhabi, U.A.E.
Alatelia Alopera, Cairo, Egypt

Selected Group Exhibitions:
1992 Cultural Foundation Exhibition Center,
Abū Dhabi, U.A.E.
1993 Royal Cultural Center, Amman, Jordan
1994 *Forces of Change: Artists of the Arab World*,
The National Museum of Women in
the Arts, Washington

Nada Raad

Born in 1943. Attended the Art Students League
in New York, and the Perugia Academy of Art in
Italy. Raad studied textile printing at the New
York Institute of Technology, and etching at the
Lebanese University. She also studied sculpture
informally with noted experts and at workshops.
She is currently living and working in Beirut,
Lebanon.

Selected Solo Exhibitions:
1983 Les Ateliers, Beirut, Lebanon
1989 Atelier Young, Carrara, Italy
1990 Alif Gallery, Washington, D.C.
La Subbia Gallery, Lido di Camaiore, Italy
1992 Le Theatre de Beyrouth, Beirut, Lebanon

Selected Group Exhibitions:
1987 *MAC 2000*, Grand Palais, Paris
1988 *Laboratorio d'Arte alla Versiwawa*, Marina
di Pietrasanta, Italy
Biblioteca Commonale, Pisanta, Italy
Mosta di Pittura e Scultura, Stabbiano, Italy
1989 *Scultura al Temminile*, La Subbia, Italy
1990 Three Contemporary Sculptors, Musée de
L'Institut du Monde Arabe, Paris
1994 *Forces of Change: Artists of the Arab World*,
The National Museum of Women in
the Arts, Washington

Khairat al-Saleh

Born in Jerusalem of Syrian parents. Received a
bachelor's degree in English literature from Cairo
University in Egypt, and a master's degree in
English drama and poetry from the University of
Wales in 1978. Al-Saleh is a poet, editor and translator. She is the author of *Fabled Cities: Princes and
Jinn from Arab Myths and Legends*. In addition to her
literary pursuits, she began to devote her time to
painting, printmaking and ceramics. She has made
detailed studies of Arabic manuscripts and ceramics at the British Museum in London.

Al-Saleh lives and works in England. Her work
is found in several public and private collections
throughout the Arab world.

Selected Solo Exhibitions:
1985 Shuruq Book Shop, Arab Women Council,
London
1992 Chelsea Old Town Hall Gallery, London
Shaftesbury Art Center, Richmond, England
1993 Royal Worcester Gallery (Rosenthal Art
Gallery), Jedda, Saudi Arabia

Selected Group Exhibitions:
1976 Arab Women Council Exhibition, World
of Islam Festival, London
1981 Chelsea Old Town Hall Gallery, London
1985/
1986 Islamic Cultural Center, London
1989 Abdul Hameed Shoman Foundation,
Amman, Jordan
Orleans House, Richmond, England

1990 GATT Gallery of the United Nations,
     Geneva, Switzerland
1991 Café Royal, London
1992 Richmond Printmakers, Ryder Court,
     London
     Royal Worcester Gallery, Jedda, Saudi
     Arabia
1994 *Forces of Change: Artists of the Arab World*,
     The National Museum of Women in
     the Arts, Washington

Zeinab Salem

Born in Ismailia, Egypt, in 1945. Received a Ph.D.
in applied arts from Essen University in Germany.
She is a member of several Egyptian arts organiza-
tions, including the Syndicate for Plastic Arts.
Salem has participated in several group exhibitions, and has received numerous awards for her
ceramic work. Her work can be found in museum
collections in Egypt.

Selected Solo Exhibitions:
1977 Royal Academy of Arts and Design, Holland
     Aki Academy of Arts, Holland
1984 Akhnaton Gallery, Cairo, Egypt
1986 Akhnaton Gallery, Cairo, Egypt
1989 Akhnaton Gallery, Cairo, Egypt

Selected Group Exhibitions:
1977 Suez Canal Authority, Ismailia, Egypt
1984 Festival of the Faculty of Fine Arts, Menia
     University, Menia, Egypt
1991 Egyptian Women, Egyptian Academy of
     Arts, Rome
1992 Egyptian Women Artists, Hall of Plastic
     Arts, Opera House, Cairo, Egypt
1993 First International Triennial of Pottery,
     Cairo, Egypt
1994 *Forces of Change: Artists of the Arab World*,
     The National Museum of Women in
     the Arts, Washington

Mona Saudi

Born in Amman, Jordan, in 1945. Graduated from
the École Supérieure des Beaux-Arts in Paris in
1973. Influenced by the art of Constantin
Brancusi, she works predominantly in stone. Saudi
has created a number of large-scale sculptures for
public spaces currently on display in Paris and
throughout Jordan. She has also participated in
many group exhibitions.

Saudi is well loved for her early publication of
drawings and writings of Palestinian children living in refugee camps in the book *In Time of War:
Children Testify (1970)*. An arts activist, she has
organized many international exhibitions in support of Palestine. She has earned a reputation
both as a sculptor and as a poet.

Having lived in Paris and Beirut, Lebanon, for
many years, Saudi has recently returned to Jordan
to establish a creative center for sculpture and the
arts. Her work is in museum collections throughout the world.

Selected Solo Exhibitions:
1963 Café de la Presse, Beirut, Lebanon
1971 Galerie Vercamer, Paris
1973 Gallery One, Beirut, Lebanon
1975 Galerie Contemporain, Beirut, Lebanon
1981 Galerie Elissar, Beirut, Lebanon
1982 Galerie Épreuve d'Artiste, Beirut, Lebanon
1983 Alia Art Gallery, Amman, Jordan
1985 Al-Salmieh Gallery, Kuwait City, Kuwait
1992 Gallery 50 × 70, Beirut, Lebanon
     Al-Balkaa Art Gallery, Fuheis, Jordan

Selected Group Exhibitions:
1983 Arab Contemporary Art, London
1987 Arab Contemporary Art, Paris
1991 Jordanian Contemporary Art, Ontario,
     Canada
1993 Atelier Art Public, Paris
1994 *Forces of Change: Artists of the Arab World*,
     The National Museum of Women in
     the Arts, Washington

Laila al-Shawa

Born in Gaza, Palestine, in 1940. Studied at the
Leonardo da Vinci School of Art in Cairo. In 1964
she received degrees from the Accademia de Belle
Arti and from the Accademia St. Giaccomo in
Rome. Studied with Oskar Kokoschka, the noted
Austrian Expressionist, in Austria.

Shawa is a painter, lecturer and illustrator of children's books. In 1988 she created stained glass
windows for the Gaza Cultural Center. A member
of the Union of Palestinian Artists, she has exhibited with the union in most Arab countries, Russia,
China, Japan, Malaysia, the United Kingdom,
Eastern Europe and the United States. She has
divided her time between London and Gaza since
1967, and currently lives in London. Her work is
in several museum collections and is found in private collections throughout the world.

Selected Solo Exhibitions:
1965 Marna House, Gaza, Palestine
1968 The Book Center Gallery, Beirut, Lebanon
1970 Hotel Vendôme, Beirut, Lebanon
1971 Dar Tunis, Beirut, Lebanon
1972 Sultan Gallery, Kuwait
1975 L'Antiquaire Gallery, Beirut, Lebanon
1976 Sultan Gallery, Kuwait City, Kuwait
1990 National Art Gallery, Amman, Jordan
1992 The Gallery, London

Selected Group Exhibitions:
1987 *Arab Women Artists in the United Kingdom*,
     Kufa Gallery, London
1988 Baghdad Biennial, Saddam Center,
     Baghdad, Iraq
1989 *Contemporary Art from the Islamic World*,
     Barbican Centre London
1990 Malaysian Experience, National Art Gallery,
     Kuala Lumpur, Malaysia
1992 Three Artists from Gaza, Abdul Hameed
     Shoman Foundation, Amman, Jordan

1993 SAGA Salon de l'Estampe et de l'Edition
d'Art a Tirage Limité, Grand Palais, Paris
1994 *Forces of Change: Artists of the Arab World,*
The National Museum of Women in
the Arts, Washington

Naima el-Shishini

Born in Guiza, Egypt, in 1929. Studied art history
at Denmark's Copenhagen University in 1970–71,
and at Istanbul University in Turkey, in 1976–77.
She received a master's degree in fine arts from
the Faculty of Fine Arts in Alexandria, Egypt,
where she now teaches.

El-Shishini is a member of the Syndicate for
Plastic Arts and the Cultural Council of the
Governor of Alexandria. Her work is included in
museum collections throughout the Arab world
and in Yugoslavia.

Selected Solo Exhibitions:
1972 Akhnaton Gallery, Cairo, Egypt
1973 International Press Club, Madrid
1974 Alexandria Atelier, Alexandria, Egypt
1977 Taksim Gallery, Istanbul, Turkey
1981 Akhnaton Gallery, Cairo, Egypt
Alexandria Atelier, Alexandria, Egypt
1983 Alexandria Atelier, Alexandria, Egypt
Akhnaton Gallery, Cairo, Egypt
1985 Boushery Gallery, Kuwait City, Kuwait
Tanagra Gallery, Alexandria, Alexandria,
Egypt
1986 Alexandria Atelier, Alexandria, Egypt
Robert Schumann Gallery, Music Academy,
Düsseldorf, Germany
1989 Alexandria Atelier, Alexandria, Egypt
Stadt Werke, Düsseldorf, Germany

Selected Group Exhibitions:
1978 Alexandria Atelier, Alexandria, Egypt
1979 The Artist and His Chosen Piece of Art,
Salem Gallery, Cairo, Egypt
1980 Alexandria Atelier, Alexandria, Egypt
1981 National Society for Fine Arts, Grand Palais,
Paris
Spring Salon, Museum of Fine Arts,
Alexandria, Egypt
1983 Art '83, American Center, Alexandria, Egypt
1985 São Paulo Biennial, São Paulo, Brazil
Faculty of Helwân University, Museum
of Fine Arts, Alexandria, Egypt
1987 The School of Alexandria, Academy of Fine
Arts, Rome
1989 Alexandrian Vision, Nile Gallery, Cairo,
Egypt
1994 *Forces of Change: Artists of the Arab World,*
The National Museum of Women in
the Arts, Washington

Suha Shoman

Born in Jerusalem in 1944. Resides in Amman,
Jordan. She studied law in Beirut, Lebanon, and
in Paris. In 1977 she joined the Fahrelnissa Zeid
Royal Institute of Fine Arts in Jordan. She is the
founder and director of Darat al-Funun in Amman,
a gallery and visual resources center library dedicated to the stimulation of the visual arts in the
Arab world.

Shoman is an active painter whose current focus is
abstractions based upon the landscape and history
of ancient Petra. Her work can be found in many
museum collections.

Selected Solo Exhibitions:
1984 *Galaxies d'Orient,* Galerie Wally Findlay,
Paris
1986 Formations by the Sea, Jordan National
Gallery of Fine Arts, Amman, Jordan
1988 The Legend of Petra, Royal Cultural
Center, Amman, Jordan
1993 The Legend of Petra II, Jordan National
Gallery of Fine Arts, Amman, Jordan

Selected Group Exhibitions:
1981 Fahrelnissa Zeid and Her Students, Palace
of Culture, Amman, Jordan
Jordan Cultural Week, Moscow
1981/
1987 Salon d'Automne, Paris (yearly)
1983 Jordanian Artists, Royal Cultural Center,
Amman, Jordan
1989 *Contemporary Art From the Islamic World,*
Barbican Centre, London
Nine Women: In Black and White, Galerie
P. Morda, Paris
1991 *Contemporary Art from Jordan,* McIntosh
Gallery, Ontario, Canada
The South of the World, Marsala, Sicily
1992 Jordanian Artists Exhibition, Spanish
Cultural Center, Amman, Jordan
1994 *Forces of Change: Artists of the Arab World,*
The National Museum of Women in
the Arts, Washington

Gazbia Sirry

Born in Egypt in 1925. For several years she was
a professor of painting on the faculty of art education of Helwân University, Cairo, Egypt, and at
the American University of Cairo. Sirry received
a bachelor's degree in fine arts and diploma in art
education in 1948 and 1949. She continued her
education abroad, studying with Marcel Gromaire
in Paris in 1951. She also studied in Italy in 1952
and in London, where she received a post-graduate degree in 1954.

In 1965 and 1975 Sirry was awarded fellowships
from the Huntington Hartford Foundation, Los
Angeles, and the Deutscher Academisher
Austauschdiest, Berlin. For six consecutive years
she received the National Creativity Grant.

Sirry has been the recipient of numerous awards,
including the Prize of Rome (1952), the Honorary
Prize for the Venice Biennial (1956) and first prize
in painting at the Alexandria Biennial (1963).
A prolific artist, she has had more than fifty solo

exhibitions in Egypt and other Arab countries, Europe, Asia, the United States and Canada.

Selected Solo Exhibitions:
1953 Modern Art Museum, Cairo, Egypt
1955 Egyptian Cultural Center, London
Cairo Atelier, Cairo, Egypt
1962/
1963 Manasterly Museum, Cairo, Egypt
1965 Gallery of Fine Arts, Ministry of Culture, Cairo, Egypt
Modern Art Museum, Alexandria, Egypt
American Friends of the Middle East, San Francisco, Calif.
Akhnaton Gallery, Cairo, Egypt (also 1968, 1973, 1985, 1987 and 1992)
1967 Gallery Brinken, Stockholm, Sweden
1968 Galerie de Centre Culturel Egyptien, Paris
Gallery One, Beirut, Lebanon
1969 Galerie La Palette Blue, Paris (also 1970)
1970 Institut Goethe, Cairo, Egypt (also 1971, 1973, 1976, 1979, 1988, and 1982)
Zaydler Gallery, London
1971 Galerie Marcel Bernheim, Paris
1972 Gallery Cultural Centre for Diplomats, Ministry of Culture, Cairo, Egypt
Dalas Exhibition Hall, Bucharest, Romania
1973 Unitarian Church Gallery, Toronto, Canada
Arts Centre Gallery, Ottawa and Montreal, Canada
1974 Middle East Institute, Washington
University of California at Los Angeles, Los Angeles
1976 Gallery Neuer Berliner Kunstverien, Berlin
1977 Galerie de Centre Culturel Egyptien, Paris
1980 Egyptian Academy, Rome
1983 Gallery Sultan, Kuwait City, Kuwait
1984 Galerie Terre du Marais, Paris
1986 Galerie el-Medina, Tunis, Tunisia
1988 Mashrabia Gallery, Cairo, Egypt
1989 Egyptian Centre for International Cultural Cooperation, Cairo
1992 Alexandria Atelier, Alexandria, Egypt
Egyptian Centre for International Cultural Cooperation, Cairo, Egypt

Selected Group Exhibitions:
1950 Modern Art Museum, Cairo, Egypt (also 1951)
1952 Group of Modern Art, Cairo and Alexandria, Egypt (also 1953)
1953 São Paulo Biennial, São Paulo, Brazil (also 1963)
1954 Eight Painters from Egypt, Galerie André Maurice, Paris
London Group, New Burlington Galleries, London
1959 Alexandria Biennial, Alexandria, Egypt (also 1961 and 1963)
1961 Permanent Exhibition of State Fellowships, Manasterly Museum, Cairo, Egypt
1967 Egypt-USA Cultural Exchange Exhibition, Cairo, Egypt
Five Artists Look at Egypt, Stockholm, Sweden (toured Sweden)

1968 State Fellowship Exhibition, Fine Arts Gallery, Cairo, Egypt
30th Anniversary: Institute of Art Education, Cairo, Egypt
1969 Exhibition of Egyptian Contemporary Art, Eastern Europe
1971 Exhibition of Egyptian Contemporary Art, Musée Galliera, Paris
1974 Exhibition of Egyptian Contemporary Art, Japan
1975 10 Egyptian Women Painters Over Half a Century, Arab Socialists Union Gallery, Cairo, Egypt
Exhibition of Egyptian Contemporary Art, Tobengen and Bonn, Germany
1978 Exhibition of Three Egyptian Artists, Galerie d'Art Mitkel, Ivory Coast
1981 *Egypt Today: 16 Contemporary Artists*, Washington, Houston, Tex. and Los Angeles, Calif.
1982 Muestra International de Arte Gráfica, Bilbao, Spain
1984 Galerie Troy, Paris
1987 Pioneer Women in Fine Arts in Egypt, Institut Goethe, Cairo, Egypt
1988 Women in Fine Arts, New Delhi, India
Baghdad International Festival of Art, Saddam Center, Baghdad, Iraq
1994 *Forces of Change: Artists of the Arab World*, The National Museum of Women in the Arts, Washington

Oumaya Alieh Soubra

Born in Beirut, Lebanon, in 1938. Received a B.A. from the American University of Beirut in 1952, and went on to obtain degrees in pharmacy and medical analysis. During the 1970s she studied art, receiving a diploma from the Academy of Beaux-Arts in Florence in 1978. Soubra is the recipient of several awards for excellence in the arts and has received substantial critical attention.

Selected Solo Exhibitions:
1972 Galerie Vendôme, Hotel Vendôme, Beirut, Lebanon
1979 Galerie Tripel-Corroy, Paris

Selected Group Exhibitions:
1980 L'Exposition International d'Aujourd'hui, Grand Palais, Paris
1982 International Festival, Château Musée, Cagnes-sur Mer, Cagnes, France
Salon d'Automne, Grand Palais, Paris
1983 Salon d'Art, Hôtel de Ville, Mantes-la-Jolie, France
1985 Contemporary Art, Foret Museum, Tokyo
1988 Feminine International Cultural Federation, Athens
1990 Painters of the 15th District, Mairie du XVè, Paris
The Lebanese Movement, UNESCO, Paris
1991 World Applied Arts Biennial, Académie Mondiale d'Information et de Docu-mentation Artistique, Lyon and Paris

1994 *Forces of Change: Artists of the Arab World,*
The National Museum of Women in
the Arts, Washington

Rabia Sukkarieh
Born in Baalbek, Lebanon, in 1953. Received a
bachelor's degree from the Fine Arts Institute in
Beirut, Lebanon, in 1984. Continuing her studies
in the United States, Sukkarieh settled in
California, where she studied communication arts
and literature at Mills College in Oakland, and
at Lutheran University. She received a master's
degree from the Art Center College of Design in
Pasadena, Calif., in 1989.

Selected Solo Exhibitions
and Performances:
1987 Art Center Auditorium, Pasadena
1988 Illusion and Women, Main Television
Station, Beirut, Lebanon
About the Death of a Hero, Hilton Hotel,
Pasadena, Calif.
Wrapping the Burned Trees, Kaskas Park,
Beirut, Lebanon
Poppies and the Garbage Alleys, Streets of
Beirut, Lebanon
1989 *Me and Them,* Art Center-Graduate Studio,
Pasadena, Calif.
1990 *Sheherezade,* Art Center Gallery, Pasadena,
Calif.
1994 Galleria Notturna, Milan, Italy

Selected Group Exhibitions
and Performances:
1984 Riyadh, Saudi Arabia
Contemporary Lebanese Artists, Beit ed-
Dein Museum, Beit ed-Dein, Lebanon
War and Peace, Streets of West Beirut,
Beirut, Lebanon
1985 Contemporary Lebanese Artists, Beit ed-
Dein Museum, Beit ed-Dein, Lebanon
1989 *Five Hundred Roses for the Shatilla Massacre,*
Art Cente Gallery, Pasadena, Calif.
1990 Opening, Galleria Notturna, Milan, Italy
1991 Spiritual Landscape, Biota Gallery, Calif.
1992/
1993 Venice Art Walk, Venice, Calif.
1994 *Forces of Change: Artists of the Arab World,*
The National Museum of Women in
the Arts, Washington

Chaibia Tallal
Born in a suburb of Casablanca, Morocco, in 1929.
A self-taught painter, she was discovered by
Moroccan artist Ahmed Cherkadh and Pierre
Gaudibert, director of the Musée d'Art Moderne,
Grenoble, France. One of her paintings was
selected as the poster for the 1984 Contemporary
Women's International Art Exhibition in Vitry-
sur-Seine, France. Tallal's works are exhibited
widely in Europe and the Arab world and are
found in private and public collections worldwide.

Selected Exhibitions:
1966 Institut Goethe, Casablanca, Morocco
Galerie Solstice, Paris
Salon des Surindépendants, Musée d'Art
Moderne de la Ville de Paris, Paris
Kunstkabinett, Frankfurt, Germany
1970 Les Halles aux Idées de Fête, Paris
1973 Galerie l'Oeil de Boeuf, Paris (also 1974,
1980, 1981, 1983, 1985, 1989)
1974 Salon des Réalités Nouvelles, Paris
Galerie Ivans Spence, Ibiza, Spain
1976 Art Biennial, Menton, France
Exposition Collective, Tunis, Tunisia
1977 Arab Biennial, Rabat, Morocco
Salon de Mai, Musée d'Art Moderne de
la Ville de Paris, Paris
Salon des Réalités Nouvelles, Paris
1978 Centre Culturel Choregraphique, Paris
(also 1980)
1979 Centre Culturel, Montmorillon, France
1980 Galerie Ibtissam, Tunis (also in 1983)
Galerie Engel, Rotterdam, The Netherlands
Galerie Ojedus, Denmark
1981 Grand Palais, Paris
1982 Galeries Raleigh, Musée Raleigh, Cagnes-
sur-Mer, Cagnes, France
1984 Exhibition, French Institute, Athens
Municipal Galerie, Vitry-sur-Seine, France
Hôtel de Ville, Yverdon, Switzerland
Les Bains, Musée d'Art, Lausanne,
Switzerland
1985 French Institute, Barcelona, Spain
Nineteen Painters of Morocco, Centre
National d'Art Contemporain, Grenoble,
France
La Maison de la Culture, Grenoble, France
Nineteen Painters of Morocco, Musée
National des Arts Africains et Océaniens,
Paris
Salon de Mai, Grand Palais, Paris (also in
1986)
1986 *Indomptés de l'Art,* Musée Granville,
Besançon, France
Galerie Moulay Ismail, Rabat, Morocco
Salon d'Automne, Grand Palais, Paris
1988 Musée d'Art Moderne de la Ville de Paris,
Paris
The African Influence Gallery, Boston,
Mass.
Five Contemporary Moroccan Artists, Gallery
Ana Izay, Beverly Hills, Calif.
1990 Neuve Invention, Collection d'Art Brut,
Lausanne, Switzerland, and Swiss
Institute, New York
Musée de l'Institut du Monde Arabe, Paris
1991 Galerie d'Art Frederic Damgaard, Syria
1994 *Forces of Change: Artists of the Arab World,*
The National Museum of Women in
the Arts, Washington

Vera Tamari
Born in Jerusalem in 1945. Graduated from the
Beirut College for Women in Lebanon in 1966.
Specialized in ceramics at the Instituto Statale per

la Ceramica in Florence, Italy, in 1972. In 1984 she received a master's of philosophy in Islamic art and architecture from Oxford University.

Tamari is currently a lecturer at Birzeit University and works in her studio in Ramalla, Palestine. She is coauthor of *Palestinian Village Home,* published in association with the British Museum in London. She also has written several specialized articles on Islamic ceramics and the art movement in the Occupied Territories.

Selected Solo Exhibitions:
1974   Jerusalem
1979   Ramallah, Palestine
1981   Ramallah, Palestine

Selected Group Exhibitions:
1980   Women Arab Artists, Baghdad, Iraq
1981   Third World Artists Exhibition, London
1986   Tallat: Palestinian Women's Art Exhibition, Jerusalem
1989/
1990   New Visions: Art from the Occupied Territories, Amman, Jordan; Salerno, Italy; Bonn and Frankfurt, Germany
1991   Ramallah, Palestine
1994   *Forces of Change: Artists of the Arab World,* The National Museum of Women in the Arts, Washington

Madiha Umar
Born in Aleppo, Syria, in 1908. Studied art at the Maria Grey Training College in London, graduating with honors in 1933. She studied and taught art in Baghdad, Iraq, during the 1930s. Continuing her training in Washington, Umar received a degree in art education from George Washington University and a master's degree in fine arts from the Corcoran School of Art in 1950.

Umar is a teacher and public lecturer as well as an active artist. She pioneered the modern use of Arabic calligraphy in abstract painting. Her work has received critical acclaim and has been included in many books on the history of art. Umar has had radio interviews on the BBC and Voice of America. She now resides in New York.

Selected Solo Exhibitions:
1949   Peabody Room, Georgetown University Library, Washington
       Abstract Painting and Arabic Calligraphy, Corcoran Gallery of Art, Washington
       Ginn Gallery, Silver Spring, Md.
1950   Arts Club, Washington
1951   Museum of Modern Art, San Francisco, Calif.
       International Orientalist Congress, University of Istanbul, Istanbul, Turkey
1954   Galerie Fritz, Beirut, Lebanon
1958   Garden Gallery, Middle East Institute, Washington
       Middle East Club, Washington

1961   University Graduates Club, Washington
1962   Friends of the Middle East, New York
1968   National Museum of Contemporary Art, Baghdad, Iraq
1971   Turkish Cultural Center, Baghdad, Iraq

Selected Group Exhibitions:
1948   *Watercolors,* National Museum of Natural History, Smithsonian Institution, Washington
1949   Corcoran Annual, Corcoran Gallery of Art, Washington
1955   Drawing and Sculpture, UNESCO, Beirut, Lebanon
1958   *Wives of the Diplomats,* T.F.A. Gallery, Washington
1960   *Arab Artists,* Middle East Institute, Washington
1968   Visual Artists of Iraq, National Museum, Baghdad, Iraq
1971   National Museum of Contemporary Art, Baghdad, Iraq
1981   *Arabic Calligraphy in Modern Art,* Iraqi Cultural Center, London
1994   *Forces of Change: Artists of the Arab World,* The National Museum of Women in the Arts, Washington

Samia Zaru
Born in Nablus, Palestine, in 1938. Graduate of the American University of Beirut and the Corcoran School of Art in Washington. She teaches art and design and is a consultant for the Department of Architecture and Fine Arts, Jordan University for Women in Amman.

Zaru has received numerous awards and prizes throughout the Arab world. An internationally recognized artist, she has exhibited widely in the Middle East, as well as in the United States, Europe and Asia. Her work is located in private and public collections worldwide, including the Vatican Museum in Rome and the White House Collection in Washington.

Selected Solo Exhibitions:
n.d.   UNESCO, Beirut
n.d.   Yarmuk University
n.d.   Jordan National Gallery, Amman, Jordan
n.d.   United Nations, Vienna and New York
n.d.   Traveling exhibition, major cities in the United States and Canada

Selected Group Exhibitions:
n.d.   Ministry of Culture, Amman, Jordan
n.d.   Women Artists of the Islamic World, World Islamic Festival, Barbican Centre, Oxford University, London
n.d.   International Sculpture Festival, Ireland
1994   *Forces of Change: Artists of the Arab World,* The National Museum of Women in the Arts, Washington

Fahrelnissa Zeid

Born in Istanbul, Turkey, in 1901; died in 1991. Studied at the Academy of Fine Arts in Istanbul from 1920 to 1923. Continued her art education at Académie Ranson in Paris in 1928. While in Paris, Zeid was well-received by her contemporaries and by such critics as Charles Estiènne.

Zeid had a long and distinguished career as a painter and art educator. Her works are in numerous museum collections worldwide. The founder of the Fahrelnissa Zeid Royal Institute of Fine Arts in Amman, Jordan, she was an inspiring role-model and mentor for many women artists throughout the Arab world.

Selected Solo Exhibitions:
1961 Galerie Dina Vierny, Paris
1964 Academy of Fine Arts, Istanbul, Turkey
     The Hittite Museum, Ankara, Turkey
1969 Galerie Katia Granoff, Paris
1972 Galerie Katia Granoff, Paris
1981 Palace of Culture, Amman, Jordan
1983 Royal Cultural Center, Amman, Jordan
1988 Ludwig Gallery, Aachen, Germany
     Ataturk Cultural Center, Istanbul, Turkey
1990 Musée de l'Institut du Monde Arabe, Paris
1992 Royal Cultural Center, Amman, Jordan

Selected Group Exhibitions:
1952 École de Paris, Galerie Babylone, Paris
1952 Museum of Contemporary Art, Bern, Switzerland
1953 Réalités Nouvelles, Galerie Dina Vierny, Paris (also in 1955)
1954 Institute of Contemporary Art, London
1955 Réalités Nouvelles, Galerie Dina Vierny, Paris
1956 Palais de Beaux-Arts, Galerie Aujourd'hui, Brussels, Belgium
     Île de l'Homme Errant, Galerie Kleber, Paris
1955/
1956 American Federation Society of Art and Graphic Society, New York
1955/
1957 Exhibition of International Graphic Art, Cincinnati Art Museum, Cincinnati, Ohio
1981 Salon d'Automne (Guest of Honor) Grand Palais, Paris
1994 *Forces of Change: Artists of the Arab World*, The National Museum of Women in the Arts, Washington

Afaf Zurayk

Born in Lebanon in 1948. Received a bachelor's degree in fine arts from the American University of Beirut in 1970, and a master's degree in fine arts from Harvard University in Cambridge, Mass., in 1972. Continuing her studies in Washington, she graduated from George Washington University in 1986 and the Corcoran School of Art in 1989.

Zurayk is an active painter who has taught at the university level. For a time she was director of the Alif Gallery in Washington. She has been an active member of the Arab American Cultural Foundation.

Selected Solo Exhibitions:
1987 Smuggler's Inn, Beirut, Lebanon
1980 Institut Goethe, Beirut, Lebanon
1987 Addison/Ripley Gallery, Washington
1991 Foundry Gallery, Washington
1993 Foundry Gallery, Washington

Selected Group Exhibitions:
1991 *All of Us*, Foundry Gallery, Washington
     Global Color, Art Barn Gallery, Washington
     Arab Women in the Arts, Alif Gallery, Washington.
     Visible Differences, Martin Luther King Library, Washington
1992 Foundry Artists Annual, Foundry Gallery, Washington
1993 Four Arab Artists from the United States, Abdul Hameed Shoman Foundation, Amman, Jordan
1994 *Forces of Change: Artists of the Arab World*, The National Museum of Women in the Arts, Washington

Mariam A. Aleem
Egyptian

"Life of an Artist"
1985
Lithograph on paper
19¹/₂ × 23¹/₂ in.
Collection of the artist

Ivonne A-Baki
Lebanese

Unity
1992
Oil on canvas
44 × 40 in.
Collection of the artist

Amna Abdalla
Sudanese

Untitled
1992
Batik on silk
7¹/₂ × 7 in.
Collection of the artist

Untitled
1992
Batik on silk
7¹/₂ × 7 in.
Collection of the artist

Zeinab Abdel Hamid
Egyptian

Haret el-Hussein
1991
Watercolor on paper
25 × 18 in.
Private collection

Etel Adnan
Lebanese

Carried with the Sound
1991
Artist's book,
watercolor and ink
on Japanese paper
Poem by Nouri
el-Jarrah
7 × 230¹/₂ in. (open)
Collection of the artist

*One Linden Tree,
Then Another . . .*
1975
Artist's book,
watercolor and ink
on Japanese paper
10¹/₂ × 248¹/₄ in. (open)
Collection of the artist

Tamam al-Akhal
Palestinian

Liberty & Democracy
1993
Oil on canvas
30 × 20 in.
Collection of the artist

Ida Alamuddin
Lebanese

Overflow
1993
Collage, charcoal
and oil
29 × 22 in.
Collection of the artist

So Below
1992
Collage, charcoal
and oil glaze
29 × 22 in.
Collection of the artist

Wijdan Ali
Jordanian

Women of Carbala
1993
Mixed media on
handmade paper
Triptych
53 × 84¹/₂ in.
Collection of the artist

Sawsan Amer
Egyptian

Icon, 1990
Mixed media on glass
19 × 21 in.
Private collection

Evelyn Ashmalla
Egyptian

Untitled
1991
Acrylic on paper
19¹/₂ × 13¹/₂ in.
Collection of the artist

Untitled
1991
Acrylic on paper
19¹/₂ × 13¹/₂ in.
Collection of the artist

Suad al-Attar
Iraqi

Legend I
1991
Oil on canvas
72 × 60 in.
Collection of the artist

*"Even the darkness . . .
shines brighter there"*
1990
Ink on paper
5 × 7 in.
Collection of the artist

*"If only I could reach you
. . . my moon, my love"*
1990
Ink on paper
5 × 7 in.
Collection of the artist

*"Together . . . we will find
a world of dreams"*
1990
Ink on paper
5 × 7 in.
Collection of the artist

Ginane Makki Bacho
Lebanese

*The Image of the Word
The Image of the Picture*
1985
Artist's book,
hand-colored prints
11¹/₂ × 15¹/₂ in.
Collection of the artist

Samira Badran
Palestinian

*Al-Dras, A Door
in Jerusalem*
1993
Acrylic on paper
49 × 43 in.
Collection of the artist

United Fire
1993
Acrylic on paper
43¹/₂ × 47 in.
Collection of the artist

Thuraya al-Baqsami
Kuwaiti

Cemetery from the East
1989
Watercolor and ink
on paper
19¹/₄ × 16 in.
Collection Jordan
National Gallery
of Fine Arts

Baya
See Baya Mahieddine

Meriem Bouderbala
Tunisian

Eclipse
1993
Mixed media on canvas
19³/₄ × 19³/₄ in.
Collection of the artist

Huguette Caland
Lebanese

Tendresse
1975
Silk
Collection of the artist

Miroir
1974
Silk
Collection of the artist

Tête à Tête
1971
Silk
Collection of the artist

Foule
1970
Silk
Collection of the artist

For all works above:
Silk fabric handwoven
by Abdulnour
(Lebanon).
Embroidery by Izzat
Attar (Syria) and Adnan
Channer (Syria).
Mannequins fabricated
in 1985 by Veronique
Daticourt (Paris).

Chaibia
See Chaibia Tallal

**Wasma'a K.
Chorbachi**
Iraqi

Profession of Faith
1991–92
Ceramic, opaque
white glaze
15 in. diameter
Collection of the artist

Profession of Faith
1991–92
Ceramic, green glazes
17 in. diameter
Collection of the artist

Saloua Raouda Choucair
Lebanese

Untitled
1983
Wood
28 × 16 × 13¹/₂ in.
Collection of the artist

Two = One
1993
Oil on cardboard
37 × 49¹/₄ in.
Collection of the artist

Two = One
1947
Oil on cardboard
24¹/₂ × 32 in.
Collection of the artist

Khulood Da'mi
Iraqi

Earth . . . Water . . . Light
1992
Stoneware
12 × 10¹/₄ × 2 in.
Collection of the artist

Earth . . . Water . . . Light
1992
Stoneware
10 in. diameter
Collection of the artist

Inji Efflatoun
Egyptian

Prison 126
1960
Oil on canvas
11³/₄ × 35¹/₂ in.
Collection Gulperie
Ismael Sabry Abdallah

Balqees Fakhro
Bahraini

Birth
1990
Acrylic
30 × 30 in.
Collection of the artist

Rima Farah
with Kevin Jackson
Syrian

Pot, 1987
Etching
32 × 36¹/₂ in.
Collection Jordan
National Gallery
of Fine Arts

Maysaloon Faraj
Iraqi

Sisters in Black and Gold, 1988
Stoneware
21¹/₂ × 11 in.
Collection Raya Jallad

Fatima Hassan el-Farouj
Moroccan

Le Mariagede Ait
1992
Mixed media on canvas
55 × 79 in.
Collection of the artist

Simone Fattal
Syrian

Sannine 1
1978
Oil on canvas
57¹/₂ × 45 in.
Collection of the artist

Amal Ftouni
Lebanese

Pattern & Women
1990
Computer generated
photograph, pixel paint
8 × 10 in.
Collection of the artist

Pattern & Women
1990
Computer generated
photograph, pixel paint
8 × 10 in.
Collection of the artist

Pattern & Women
1990
Computer generated
photograph, pixel paint
8 × 10 in.
Collection of the artist

Pattern & Women
1990
Computer generated
photograph, pixel paint
8 × 10 in.
Collection of the artist

Pattern & Women
1990
Computer generated
photograph, pixel paint
8 × 10 in.
Collection of the artist

Lina Ghaibeh
Syrian

Death of Time
1992
Computer generated
photograph
7¹/₄ × 9 in.
Collection of the artist

Going Under
1992
Computer generated
photograph
6¹/₄ × 9 in.
Collection of the artist

Burning City
1992
Computer generated
photograph
6 × 9 in.
Collection of the artist

Metamorphosis
1992
Computer generated
photograph
6¹/₄ × 9 in.
Collection of the artist

Riham Ghassib
Jordanian

Al-SALT
1993
Watercolor
38¹/₂ × 38¹/₂ in.
Private collection

Samia Halaby
Palestinian

Fertilization
1993
Oil on canvas
36 × 48 in.
Collection of the artist

Variable Motion
1993
Oil on canvas
36 × 46 in.
Collection of the artist

Tahia Halim
Egyptian

Untitled
1978
Oil on canvas
24 × 19¹/₂ in.
Collection Mr. and
Mrs. Esmat Halawa

Mona Hatoum
Palestinian

Untitled
1992
Wire mesh
38¹/₂ × 17¹/₂ × 28 in.
Collection of the artist

Fawzia el-Hicheri
Tunisian

Homage to Paul Klee
1991
Woodcut
98¹/₂ × 59 in.
Collection of the artist

Nabila Hilmi
Palestinian

People Series
1993
Mixed media on paper
9 × 12 in.
Collection of the artist

People Series
1993
Mixed media on paper
9 × 12 in.
Collection of the artist

People Series
1993
Mixed media on paper
9 × 12 in.
Collection of the artist

People Series
1993
Mixed media on paper
9 × 12 in.
Collection of the artist

Jumana el-Husseini
Palestinian

Untitled
1991
Mixed media on paper
30¹/₂ × 22¹/₂ in.
Collection His Royal
Highness Prince Talal
Bin Mohammad

Untitled
1991
Mixed media
30¹/₂ × 22¹/₂ in.
Collection Nazir al-Sati

Kamala Ishaq Ibrahim
Sudanese

Loneliness
1987
Oil on canvas
41 × 41 in.
Collection Jordan
National Gallery
of Fine Arts

Siham Abu Acle Jaar
Palestinian

Anthuriums
1986
Oil on canvas
28 3/4 × 23 1/2 in.
Collection of the artist

Ghada Jamal
Lebanese

Cloud Burst Series 2
1991
Oil on paper
12 1/2 × 14 3/4 in.
Collection of the artist

Cloud Burst Series 5
1991
Oil on paper
12 1/2 × 14 3/4 in.
Collection of the artist

Cloud Burst Series 7
1991
Oil on paper
14 1/2 × 15 3/4 in.
Collection of artist

Cloud Burst Series 8
1991
Oil on paper
12 1/2 × 14 3/4 in.
Collection of the artist

Lebanon Cityscape: Sad Streets, Frightened Eyes
1990
Oil on paper
60 × 40 in.
Collection Jack Shea

To Everything There Is a Season
1989
Artist's book, mixed media
8 × 12 in.
Collection Dr. and Mrs. Frank Agrama

Liliane Karnouk
Egyptian

Black & Green
1992
Installation
Eight photographic collages
17 3/4 × 11 1/2 in. each
Three mixed media on canvas panels
89 1/4 × 58 in. each

Six photographic collages with birch bark and acrylic
17 1/2 × 12 1/2 in.
17 1/4 × 12 1/4 in.
21 1/4 × 12 1/2 in.
23 × 17 in.
21 1/2 × 16 1/2 in.
17 1/2 × 13 1/2 in.
Collection of the artist

Leila Kawash
Iraqi

Diaspora
1992
Mixed media collage on canvas
36 × 30 in.
Collection of the artist

Helen Khal
Lebanese

Horizon of Peace
1986
Oil on canvas
39 1/2 × 49 1/4 in.
Collection of the artist

Sabiha Khemir
Tunisian

Confrontation
1993
Ink on paper
8 1/2 × 12 in.
Collection of the artist

Shipwreck 2
1993
Ink on paper
8 1/2 × 12 in.
Collection of the artist

Nazli Madkour
Egyptian

Oasis, 1990
Mixed media and papyrus on canvas
39 1/2 × 39 1/2
Collection of the artist

Baya Mahieddine
Algerian

Femmes Portant de Coupes
1966
Gouache on paper
39 1/2 × 59 in.
Collection L'Institut du Monde Arabe

Nadira Mahmoud
Omani

Untitled
1990
Acrylic on paper
24 1/2 × 29 1/2 in.
Collection Jordan National Gallery of Fine Arts

Seta Manoukian
Lebanese

Willing to Begin
1990
Acrylic on canvas
82 × 70 in.
Collection of the artist

Rima Mardam-Bey
Syrian

Dreams 1
1991
Charcoal and acrylic
61 × 34 in.
Collection of the artist

Dreams 2
1991
Charcoal and acrylic
61 × 34
Collection of the artist

Dreams 3
1991
Charcoal and acrylic
61 × 34
Collection of the artist

Mounirah Mosly
Saudi Arabian

May You One Day Hear the Cry of a Window Being Born into the World 1
1991–92
Mixed media on tent fabric with collage
55 × 58 in.
Collection of the artist

May You One Day Hear the Cry of a Window Being Born into the World 2
1991–92
Mixed media on tent fabric with collage
47 × 31 in.
Collection of the artist

May You One Day Hear the Cry of a Window Being Born into the World 3
1991–92
Mixed media on tent fabric with collage
62 1/2 × 60 in.
Collection of the artist

May You One Day Hear the Cry of a Window Being Born into the World 4
1991–92
Mixed media on tent fabric with collage
44 × 38 1/2 in.
Collection of the artist

Layla Muraywid
Syrian

Contemporary Icon 25
1993
Mixed media
26 × 36 1/2 in.
Collection of the artist

Contemporary Icon 6
1993
Mixed media
22 1/2 × 16 in.
Collection of the artist

Effat Nagui
Egyptian

Icon of the Nile
1991
Mixed media on wood
68 1/2 × 43 1/2 in.
Collection of the artist

Marguerite Nakhle
Egyptian

The Bath
1953
Oil on canvas
32 × 39 1/2 in.
Collection Mr. and Mrs. Esmat Halawa

Hind Nasser
Jordanian

Mother Earth - Protege
1992
Oil on cotton
39 1/2 × 27 1/2 in.
Collection of the artist

Mother Earth - Protected
1992
Oil on cotton
$39^{1/2} \times 27^{1/2}$ in.
Collection of the artist

Rabab Nemr
Egyptian

Untitled
1985
Oil on wood
$49 \times 38^{1/2}$ in.
Collection Jordan
National Gallery
of Fine Arts

Houria Niati
Algerian

No to Torture
1982–93
Installation
Five oil on canvas
panels (1982–83)
$71^{1/2} \times 108^{1/2}$ in. (1)
and $71^{1/2} \times 53$ in. (4)
Three oil on canvas
panels (1993)
$41^{1/2} \times 35^{1/2}$ in. each
Collection of the artist

Maisoon Saqr al-Qasimi
United Arab Emirates

Narration in the Course of Its Form
1993
$27^{1/2} \times 19^{3/4}$ in.
Collection of the artist

Nada Raad
Syrian

Masque
1990
Bronze
$15^{3/4} \times 13 \times 6$ in.
Base: $29 \times 14 \times 7$ in.
Collection Jan M. Lilac

Khairat al-Saleh
Syrian

The Creation 2
1989
Gouache, gold leaf
and ink on paper
$18 \times 27^{1/2}$ in.
Collection Suha
Shoman

Zeinab Salem
Egyptian

Untitled
1990
Ceramic
$14^{1/2} \times 19$ in.
Collection of the artist

Mona Saudi
Jordanian

Formation
1992
Limestone
$15^{3/4} \times 12 \times 4$ in.
Collection of the artist

Lovers' Tree
1977
Ink and watercolor
$45 \times 35^{1/2}$ in.
Collection of the artist

Laila al-Shawa
Palestinian

Wall of Gaza
1992
Installation
Ten silkscreens
38×59 in. each
Collection of the artist

Naima el-Shishini
Egyptian

Untitled
1980
Oil on canvas
$38^{1/2} \times 38^{1/2}$ in.
Collection of the artist

Suha Shoman
Jordanian

Legend of Petra
1989
Oil on canvas
Triptych
79×59 in. each
Collection of the artist

Gazbia Sirry
Egyptian

The Couple
1993
Oil on canvas
$29^{1/2} \times 39^{1/2}$ in.
Collection of the artist

The Promenade
1993
Oil on canvas
$29^{1/2} \times 39^{1/2}$ in.
Collection of the artist

Untitled
1993
Oil on canvas
$29^{1/2} \times 39^{1/2}$ in.
Collection of the artist

Oumaya Alieh Soubra
Lebanese

Espace Lumière
1992
Oil on Japanese paper
$23^{1/2} \times 35^{1/2}$ in.
Collection of the artist

Rabia Sukkarieh
Lebanese

Sheherezade 101
1989
Installation
One hundred and one
mixed media panels,
arranged in five rows
15×15 in. each
Collection of the artist

Chaibia Tallal
Moroccan

Village de Chtouka
1982
Oil on canvas
71×71 in.
Collection L'Institut
du Monde Arabe

Vera Tamari
Palestinian

Rhythms of the Past
1993
Ceramic
$9^{1/2} \times 6$ in.
Collection of the artist

Madiha Umar
Iraqi

At the Concert
1948
Ink on white
scratch board
$9^{1/2} \times 13$ in.
Collection Hala Kitani

Wijdan
See Wijdan Ali

Samia Zaru
Palestinian

Untitled
1991
Mixed media on wood
34×31 in.
Collection of the artist

Fahrelnissa Zeid
Jordanian

Paleocristalos
1965
Sculpture
$21^{1/4} \times 13 \times 10$ in.
Collection estate of
Her Royal Highness
Princess F. Zeid

The Reverse
1964
Oil on canvas and wood
$52^{3/4} \times 65$ in.
Collection Errol Karim
Aksoy Foundation

Afaf Zurayk
Lebanese

Recollections
1993
Fourteen mixed media
drawings on paper
$8 \times 8^{1/2}$ in. each
Collection of the artist